Sp

A Soul-Splinter Experiences Earth

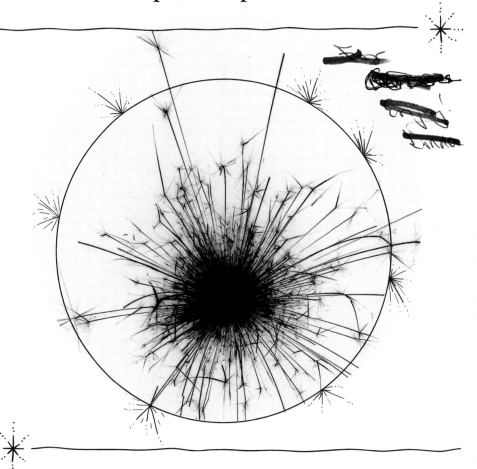

We call those poets who are first to mark
Through Earth's dull mist the coming of the dawn,
Who see in twilight's gloom the first pale spark,
While others only note that day is done.
Oliver Wendell Holmes Sr.

Linda Varsell Smith

Thanks to

Maureen Frank: The Mandala Lady
for preparing the manuscript for printing
and designing the covers and illustrations.
www.TheMandalaLady.com

My poetry friends, critique groups,
intuitive consultants and family.

© Copyright 2017 by Rainbow Communications

ISBN:978-0-9888554-5-8

Rainbow Communications
471 NW Hemlock Avenue
Corvallis, OR 97330

varsell4@comcast.net

Linda Varsell Smith sparks creativity as a teacher, poet, and novelist.
She sparkles in Corvallis, Oregon with her husband Court
in a mini-museum sparkling with miniature collections.
She sparked creative writing, children's literature,
and literary publication at Linn-Benton Community College,
now teaching Write Your Life Story and poetry workshops.
Linda sparkled with enthusiasm for 32 years as a Calyx Books editor
and the Eloquent Umbrella literary magazine advisor.
She is sparky as president of Portland Pen Women
and former president of Oregon Poetry Association.
She is a sparkler in several writing groups,
plays competitive and cooperative Scrabble
with sparkier Scrabblers.

Table of Contents

From a little spark may burst a flame. Dante Alighieri

Spark Me

And so our mothers and grandmothers have more often than not anonymously, handed on the creative spark, the seed of the flower they themselves never hoped to see --or like a sealed letter they could not plainly read. Alice Walker

Soul-Sparks

It's about cosmic energy, a little spark of which is inside every individual as the soul. Bharati Mukherjee

Dancing Sparks

We need only stay close. In time, sparks will fly.   J. Cole

Grounding Sparks

...the radiant dandelion, like a spark dropped from the sun. Henry Ward Beecher

Sparkling Water

There are no accidents, only nature throwing her weight around...Nuclear war would be just a spark in the grandeur of space...Nature will pick up the cards we have spilled, shuffle them, and begin her game again. Camille Paglia

Spark Flight

Just as energy is the basis of life itself, and ideas the source of innovation, so is innovation the vital spark of all human change, improvement or progress. Ted Levitt

Spark Ancient Mysteries

Curiosity is the spark behind the spark of every great idea.
The future belongs to the curious. Unknown

Guardian Sparks

Instead of relying on a situation to turn around on its own, be the positive spark
that a situation needs to change from negative to positive. Anuray Prakesh Ray

Cosmic Sparks

Google the name Prometheus, and see how often it has been given to innovations in many different fields, notably science, medicine and space exploration. The fire he stole can be seen too as the spark generating all artistic creativity. Neil MacGregor

Spark Me

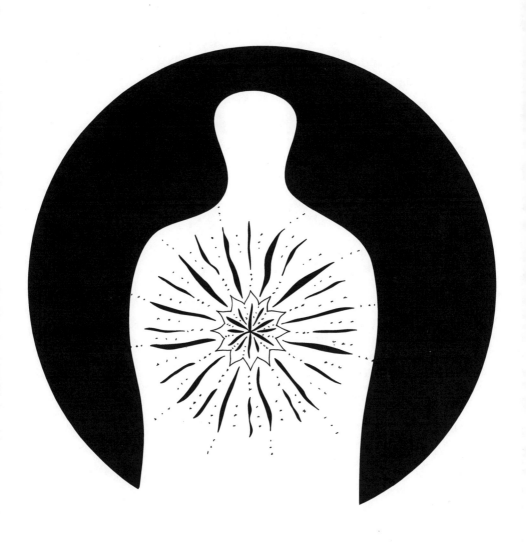

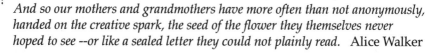

And so our mothers and grandmothers have more often than not anonymously, handed on the creative spark, the seed of the flower they themselves never hoped to see --or like a sealed letter they could not plainly read. Alice Walker

Cosmicality

My outlook might be called cosmicality
blends beyond science and spirituality.
My understanding of earthly reality
might not reflect cosmic actuality.

My interests are pierian.
harmonic and equalitarian.
I could be a Blue Ray Pleiadian,
posing as red, white and blue American.

I'm told I'm multidimensional,
my stay on Earth is intentional
like everyone, a cosmic original
currently karmically reincarnational.

I'm a benign radical
lured toward the magical
not so much the technical
believes each of us is special.

Filled with chimerical curiosity,
passionate for knowledge and creativity,
I strive to express positivity.
3D experience was a necessity.

Not sure what I was thinking of
to be in an experiment about love.
I needed a forceful shove,
promised guidance from above

Earth is this life's destination.
I needed intense orientation.
to accept this designation
with enthusiastic participation.

To live in the physical
lured to astrophysical
is probably very typical
if one dwells in the cosmical.

My thoughts come not just from senses.
It is my probable consensus
other-dimensional entities dissolve pretenses
as I challenge what life dispenses.

When I look at my situation as a whole,
I think I play a cosmically-connected role.
There is a lot of distracting rigamarole,
trying to reach for some elusive goal.

I must be some multiversal visitor,
sent to be an Earth monitor–
a humanoid bio-bot transistor
reporting to some inquisitor.

Cosmicality suggests surreality
while I deal with this locality,
has a certain practicality
as I ponder universal totality.

I Just Don't Know

I don't know how to play
this game of life in a clear way.
Is the game just win or lose?
If I'm on a team, can I choose?
The rules are elusive. I don't know why.

I don't know what guidelines are best.
Is life an experiment with exit test?
How many soul-splinters do I juggle?
Why is there a need to struggle?
Dual reality, 3D is hard. I don't know why.

I don't know how the universe started.
When was sentience imparted?
What is the meaning behind the cosmic plan?
What is my role? Do what I can?
But what is the reason? I don't know why.

I don't know expectations for bio-genetic forms
and what energy codes the norms.
What diverse kinds of consciousness exist?
Of what does this knowledge consist?
If all is One–how come I don't know why?

Feeling Blue

There are so many connotations of blue--
positive thoughts not just depression.
Not just an attitude, but helper to you.
Blue makes a positive impression.
    I'll give blue an upbeat choice.
    Stop wallowing, rejoice!

Positive thoughts not just depression
like rescuer, friend in need.
lead us in a lighter progression
Blue's a giver not taker indeed.
    Blue is a safe, non-threatening color,
    some hold blue in holy honor.

Not just an attitude, but helper to you,
you can think of robin's eggs and tranquil sky.
Your mood soars with a bluish hue,
you feel comforted and don't know why.
    Blue is an uplifter of spirit,
    an energizing benefit.

Blue makes a positive impression
when worn, expresses hope when sung.
Tones of blue in any session
can mean sadness has been flung.
    When darkness shrouds light,
    I seek black turn to blue---bright.

I'll give blue an upbeat choice
as a spark to love and my soul.
Blue chakra is center of my voice.
Blue cloaks me for a caring role.
    So as I write this restraining tears,
    perhaps blue angel wings tip my ears.

Stop wallowing, rejoice?
I came here to play, support, create.
I have not received my final invoice,
so I have cause to celebrate.
    I accept my responsibility
    for any blues inside of me.

Goal-Oriented Women

A busy, vibrant, goal-oriented woman is so much more attractive than a woman who waits around for a man to validate her existence. Mandy Hale

The first time I saw Gloria Steinum
up close from the second row
was at a League of Women Voters
National Convention in Atlanta in the 70's.

She had the large sunglasses
and long locks, unlocking hearts
and minds. She said most women
are one man away from welfare.

Even though I was happily married
with three children, I was not the chief
breadwinner and worked part-time.
I went back to school again to be prepared.

My mother called me too competitive
because I wanted to use my college degree
to teach not stay home like she did.
But with young children, I went back to get a Masters.

While my husband studied for his Ph.D,
I was expected to PHT - Put Hubby Through.
We had meetings for many working wives
without even a B.A. -- as smart or smarter than hubby.

Many of these wives were left behind
for the trophy or higher-educated wife.
They learned too late to keep
no more than one degree less than spouse.

After reading feminist literature,
I devoted over 30 years to Calyx Books
promoting women's creativity,
while teaching and writing.

We still struggle with sexism, racism, agism
and the many ism's that schism people.
We need goal-oriented visionaries to see
isms do not limit opportunity and equality.

Curiosity Buying

I do a lot of curiosity buying...anything that sparks my imagination. Bruce Springsteen

Curiosity shopping leads to curiosity buying
I don't purchase just from stores.
I select with creative trying
to find whatever imagination explores.
>My niches expand in science and art.
>until the closets in my mind fall apart.

I don't purchase just from stores.
Occasionally I browse the Internet,
but I prefer info items my bookshelf ignores.
I don't buy what's tangible on-line much yet.
>Curiosity leads and guides research.
>Curiosity often leaves me in the lurch.

I select with creative trying
personal and household needs.
For ideas I am prying
books or computer leads.
>Curiouser and curiouser like Lewis Carrol
>I wear out brain and apparel.

To find whatever imagination explores
I need images, ideas, words, sounds
to gather before my assemblage pours
onto page, screen, my stash compounds.
>Curious energy is without ends.
>Upon it all creation depends.

My niches expand in science and art
other categories get more than a glance.
At times I don't know where to start
and give new approaches a chance.
>I'm a curious omnivore,
>a cosmic terpsichore.

Until the closets in my mind fall apart
and my shopping and buying are open and free,
I'll search every gizmo and mart to jumpstart
and energize my unsatiable curiosity.
>It takes more than synergy:
>shop 'til you drop energy.

The Energetic Hitch-hiker

Sitting In facing chairs, the shaman and I
were doing sound healing with brass bowls
when the shaman noticed a spirit being
watching us from a nearby chair.

The shaman paused and described
an ephemeral form dressed
rather sparkly and garishly.
Not a classic angel type.

The shaman could not determine
gender which I said did not matter
I just wondered what this unseen energy
wanted with me. What was its purpose?

The shaman asked if I knew its name?
I said no, maybe cosmic chum?
This made the entity chuckle
and said that was fine.

When I asked if it brought recent nightmares,
and it said yes to get my attention.
Then I became suspicious and asked why
would a good-intentioned spirit do that?

Did the spirit wake me up the previous night
about three and not let me go back to sleep
until I had the rough draft of a trente-sei?
The unnamed spirit laughed yes. For me poor timing.

The shaman consulted my higher self
for clarity as he was skeptical of these intentions also.
Despite the spirit's claims it was here with sparks of humor
for my highest good, a higher honcho swished it away.

The shaman said the spirit was with me about ten days,
energetically hitch-hiking on my light.
A surprising, more positive placement would arrive
in about a week to help me with my poetry.

Metaphysically I've read about all kinds
of drop-ins, walk-ins, soul-exchanges, ghosts
diverse light and dark multi-dimensional beings.
I wish I could spot dark ones myself, blow them away.

The Bell-Ringers

Two cherubically-smiling young ladies
rang the doorbell, drew me to the door.
Cross-carrying, Christ-caddies
wanted to spread Jesus' message once more.
       My mother would invite them in.
       She fed them like the next of kin.

Rang the doorbell, drew me to the door
when I had just laid down to nap.
I did not let them in as I've done before.
They were gone in a finger-snap.
       I admire their courage of belief
       and hope their servitude is brief.

Cross-carrying, Christ caddies
are more often in the male club.
Women don't get to be higher-robed-claddies.
This snub therein lies some of my rub.
       Women get a less powerful role
       in all this sacred rigmarole.

Wanted to spread Jesus's message once more
to an elderly angel collector- easy target?
But they won't get to persuade this senior.
I smile, close the door without regret.
       Feeling softened from my massage,
       yet my sympathy for them didn't assuage.

My mother would invite them in,
sweetly feed them, attack church hierarchy.
The missionaries found to their chagrin
she considered their views pure malarkey.
       Hungry people away from family and home,
       needed sustenance, comfort of om.

She fed them like next of kin
for all are connected, seek for care.
As I wait for my rest to begin,
I realize I did not do my share.
       Wherever they come from, I can't tell.
       Just hope we all don't end up in hell.

Why I Like Angels

I can imagine angels any way I want.
      I believe I can do this multidimensionally.

Angels are luminous guardians, lightening lives,
      giving the rooted, wings.

Halos are multi-purpose: hula hoops, roll over clouds,
      headlights, a dunk hoop for orbs.

Garb does not have to be white or plain.
      Can be pants. I like blue with trim and designs.

Angels control their density- manifest physically when needed
      or stay ephemeral in less dense dimensions. I like their levity.

Supposedly we have several angelic guides. I am learning
      their names. I can call and hope they hear me.

I believe an angel saved me once from a fatal fall
      so I could complete my life.

I appreciate they resonate with the music of the spheres,
      part of the connectedness of ALL.

I collect them in many media and several sizes
      for their beauty, lightness of being, muse-ful quality.

Angels guard us since birth, whisper better intentions,
      pick us up when we stumble.

My thoughts fly with angels,
      my heart beats to their vibes.

With angels by your side, whether you sense them or not,
      it is comforting to think someone always has your back
         and attaches wings.

Healing Vibrations

Evenings when I go to sleep
I may have 14 unseen angels
        but instead of lullabies
to get their attention
for my safe keeping,
        I am trying the energies
from music and color for healing vibrations.

The goal is as I listen,
eyes closed and breathing deeply
        to make contact with these energies
to achieve a sense of well-being,
balance and inner peace.
        Sometimes I fall asleep.

The music aligns with the colors
of the seven chakras.
        As the music and color sequence
gets inhaled, my body
is supposed to vibrate, heal to glow.
        Body parts resonate. But
my visualization skills need help.

Red or the root chakra relates to fear,
survival, money, stability, security.
        The root of anxieties.

Orange is reproduction system,
sexuality, creativity.
        Procreative and creative- hmm

Yellow is personal power.
The solar plexus.
        Is this gut reaction?

Green is the heart, heart opening
Green as in growing, burgeoning.
       Why are valentine hearts red?

Blue is for the voice, throat.
self-expression. My favorite color
       is for speaking my experiences.

Indigo is the third eye, clairvoyant seeing.
My third eye may wink at me, but is not open fully.
       Sometimes I have inklings of its presence.

White is the crown chakra of my head.
This is divine knowing. I can envision white.
       Glimpse of angel wings? Head in clouds?

I try to avoid negative, low vibration colors
like gray, black, muddy brown and wimpy yellows
       and pea greens.   Not colors I like to deal with.
I ask for no nightmares, no dark entities
I press the CD button and surround myself
       with strange sounds and colors
ancient healing concepts used around the world.

Somehow as I am breathing, conjuring color,
the healing vibrations do not seem to travel
       to my very painful knees... and I can't
get on my knees to pray about it.

Stepping on Toes

God gave you toes as a device for finding furniture in the dark.
Murphy's Lesser Known Law s

My new pine double tall captain's bed
has twelve handy storage drawers.
With my new comfy mattress
I'm 33 inches above the floor.

First I borrowed a metal ladder
splattered and dribbled with paint.
It has a grasping feature
but cumbersome, my complaint.

Then I bought wooden two-step-storage-stairs
which holds two pairs of shoes,
but as I climbed into bed
I'd bump and gain a new bruise.

When I launched in the dark
toes bashed into nearby wood.
Slippery socks offered no protection
I soon sorely understood.

As I catapult and plunk on the bed
now barefoot toes grip more tightly.
When I lurch to my lofty perch,
I turn on the light, nightly.

Healing Alliance

Nightly, I high-jump onto my lofty storage bed,
      rearrange pillows for my head and under my knees.
          After I place my pillow props, flake my arms
              on the quilt or under if chilled,
            I turn off the light.

The monotone meditation tape drones, guru urges me
      to make myself comfortable, close my eyes,
          breathe deeply and relax, listen to the music
              of some exotic instrument, breathe
                for a healthier, state of mind.

I find a position I can remain in for a while,
      pay attention to patterns, color codes encoding healing,
          notice the subtle changes in wordless musical score.
              The contrast of flat voice and twanging tones
              bores or hypnotizes me.

Then I'll absorb color vibrations my inner body knows will dance
      with consciousness in a kaleidoscopic experience.
          Sound and color sensations flow through me, resonate,
              opening the body to higher consciousness
                for health, well-being and balance.

All this vibrating, inhaling, relaxing, deep breathing
      supposedly cleanses organs and functions,
          gently dissolves and releases blockages,
              I am bathed in light and sound,
                wait for beneficial effects of frequencies.

Red, orange, yellow, green, light blue, indigo, violet, white
      chakra colors come and go. In the flow until I glow,
          entering mind, body and spirit to heal
              in a higher state of consciousness,
                clearer state of being...hopefully

or until I fall asleep often after blue–my favorite color.
      If I stay awake to the end, open my eyes, I know
          I am in for a long, dark night in this painful dimension--
              not the dream dimension where there is a possibility
                my muse or angelic guides might heal me.

Learning to Downshift

I know when to go out, and when to stay in. Get things done. David Bowie

In the middle of the night I awake
gasping for air, a hot potato baked.
       What is going on?

Does a heart attack heat you to the core?
Slowly, I breathe and cool once more.
       What is going on?

If I breathe hard when in bed should I fly?
Pitch plane for train? I wonder why.
       What is going on?

I put on my color/sound meditation CD
to heal what might be wrong with me.
       What is going on?

Next day I explain this to my shaman friend.
Will life's mystery never end?
       What is going on?

It seems I travel inter-dimensionally
and I was downshifting my frequency.
       That's what's going on?

I know I've tried to raise my vibration,
but where was this destination?
       Could that be what's going on?

He explains he's experienced these hot spots.
So putting together the cosmic dots
       this could be what's going on.

But on Earth see a doctor to insure
that is the problem to be sure
       that is what is going on.

I should know when to go out
and when to stay in. Without a doubt
       something is going on.

To get the job done I need to know
when to speed and when to slow--
       flow with what is going on.

Specstarcular Prosetry

My cousin called my writing "specstarcular prosetry"
because of my unusual subjects and style.
"Masterful use of words in prose and poetry."
I just like to make people think and smile.
      Writing evokes a certain texture.
      Writing opens us to conjecture.

Because of my unusual subjects and style
I tend to startle and fall between cracks,
require readers to ponder awhile.
Cultural norms endure attacks.
      Much of what is known is theory.
      I like to explore cosmic mystery.

"Masterful use of words in prose and poetry"
may be a bit of an exaggeration,
but I aim for word-play and synergy,
try to stretch mind and imagination.
      I may cause some confusion
      as I resist a final conclusion.

I just like to make people think and smile
as I speculate on science and spirituality,
to reconcile, rile, beguile remain versatile
to prepare for possible eventuality.
      I like to word-dance and try forms,
      question rules on what conforms.

Writing evokes a certain texture,
a certain rhythm, page format.
Writers explore with sense of adventure,
can raise and lower the thermostat.
      Poets control lines tersely,
      trying to express diversely.

Writing opens us to conjecture
upon sources of love and light
bearing our soulful signature
of our multiversal insight.
      Each of us has a special voice
      to evaluate and make a choice.

One of the System Busters

You are never too old to set another goal or dream a new dream. C.S. Lewis

My goal is to be a renegade of light,
a Pleiadean Blue Ray streaming poetry
from spiritual and cosmic awakenings, despite
not reaching the vibrational level for me
      to achieve this goal in this dimension.
      All beliefs and theories in suspension.

A Pleiadean Blue Ray streaming poetry
from my innermost discoveries
unfolds some of life's mystery
from part of my recoveries.
      I know we are not alone in this multiverse.
      I want to say we are soul-splinters...in verse.

From spiritual and cosmic awakenings, despite
still trodding and plodding my life's path
creating my individual beliefs, not finding respite
from traditional religions, the aftermath
      is imagining my own Creator, finding
      the divine is within us–eternally binding.

Not reaching the vibrational level for me
to understand multi-dimensional realms,
I ponder this heavy, dark, duality, reality,
despite my trepidations and qualms.
      Somehow I find myself living here
      to bring light and to reduce fear.

To achieve this goal in this dimension
utilizing limited equipment in my quest,
regarding supposedly free will with apprehension,
yet striving to creatively do my light-hearted best,
      is one soul-splintering task.
      Love is all I ask.

All beliefs and theories in suspension
lets me explore more and not commit
to anything that could reduce my comprehension,
keeps me open and will permit
      me to enjoy my dances with word-play
      and find partners on my way.

Nailing It

A poem knows where you already are and it nails you there. William Stafford

Each letter or each word points,
spikes each line, impales it,
but first drafts are not nailed down.
I'll revise until effort pounds it.

A poem launches you
from where you are, but
is a temporary trajectory
toward new ways to input.

Form or free verse–any expression
nailing thoughts to surface
helps poet and reader to know
the purpose of this artifice.

Perhaps a poet prefers glue
to make connections
or other adhesive to capture thought
to make chosen word selections.

Few of my poems are truly fastened.
Hopefully they can wiggle, slip free
to explore where I could go.
Can you nail down curiosity?

Nail it if it works or tightens
Pry poems open for new revelations.
Nail down what is hammered out
to nail life's celebrations.

IN

Composing the Blues

I merely took the energy it takes to pout and wrote some blues. Duke Ellington

Many of my recent poems are bruised blues,
poems of protest and diminishing hope.
I'd like lines with more rainbow hues–
some resolutions and ways to cope.
> When I feel inclined to pout,
> I'll open lips to let light out.

Poems of protest, diminishing hope
seem relevant in these extreme times.
The stress pressures one to mope,
adapt attitudes as change primes.
> If poetry reflects this reality,
> will we escape to surreality?

I'd like some lines with rainbow hues,
funny, informative–maybe enlightens?
With word-play, experiments, sustainable clues
expressing compassion for what frightens.
> Poems to uplift minds and spirit
> Poems to clarify and intuit.

Some resolutions and ways to cope
in a world struggling with alienation
are beyond this poet's limited scope
to advocate for connection and cooperation.
> How can I express combative writing
> and remain non-violently fighting?

When I feel inclined to pout,
petulant, seething with anger,
I know to free my mouth to shout
when good ideas seem in danger.
> Current changes need new ideas,
> sharing insights on many medias.

I'll open lips to let light out.
When sparked within by creativity,
I'll investigate what the fuss is about
and respond with forceful positivity.
> Blue's my favorite color, by golly–
> not to be depressed by melancholy!

Poetry in the Supermarket

Three women with variously-gray hair
waited in line at the check-out.
The woman before me put
the black plastic bar between
our groceries with apologies.
"I just am out there most of the time."

I smiled and said "I'm a poet
I am out there most of the time too."
I explained it was National Poetry Month
and I had taken the challenge
of writing a poem a day.

As I placed down the bar
for the shopper behind me, she said
"I have given up listening to the news.
I'd like a poetry channel."
We all agreed and as I left the store
to channel my next poem,
I thought of ways we could have more
poetry in the supermarket.

At least for April, don't make it
Eliot's cruelest month,
or the experts calling April
the beginning of "the killing season".
Why should burgeoning spring
trigger such violence?
Why not peaceful poetry
starting with each of us.

We could sustain ourselves
strolling the colorful aisles.
What about poems read instead
of music over the sound system,
a poetry bin full of free poems
donated by local poets, poems on labels.
Imagine produce lined up as letters on shelves ,
the black bars reminders for stanza breaks,
or a new poem on the poetry conveyor belt,
shoppers smiling filling their carts with poetry,
clerks sprouting couplets and haiku,
poems along with coupons on receipt?

A solitary black bird on the dark asphalt
watches me load my shining blue Fit,
cloth bags bulging with poetry.
We are ready to fly... out there.

To Mix In Time with May Swenson

May's poetry is full of moments of interplay–perceptual games and experiments in seeing, which are grounded in a serious theory of knowledge....I don't know where May is now, but her poems continue to mix in time, and be part of the vitality of the world.　　　Richard Wilbur

Perhaps in Half Sun Half Sleep
　　　　I can raise my frequency
　　　　　　　and make contact with May
　　　　　　　　　　in the dimension she's residing.
I am supposedly multi-dimensional.
　　　　If so, we just may not have met...yet.

Since supposedly I leave my body
　　　　in the dream state–even have a starship,
I could set the intention of finding her.
　　　　I can adjust my social media outlets
　　　　and my GPS cosmically.
Voila!　Maybe a vibrational channel she senses.

She is released from Earth, A Cage of Spines.
　　　　If we are both in different forms
　　　　　　　or formless–direct contact could be iffy.
One could be pure light.　　Most likely
　　　　both have lighter bodies than on Earth,
　　　　　　　when we cruise the cosmos.

Away from this world of Windows and Stones,
I could invite her to my starship.
　　　　We could become holograms
　　　　　　　and land on the planet of our choice.

Body density, composition and vibrations
could take some tinkering.
　　　　Since everything is energy
　　　　and everything has consciousness
I can envision Things Taking Place
　　　　somewhere in space/time.

I saw her read with William Stafford
       at the New York City Y in the late 70's.
Perhaps May and Bill have reunited
       at a poetry gathering in the multiverse
          To Mix With Time.

In case I do have an encounter with May
       What would I say?
I don't want to be a gushy, starstruck fan
       wanting to be illuminated by her starshine,
I want to play with Poems to Solve,
       color The Guess and Spell Coloring Book
          create Iconographs.
I want to know what she is doing now,
       who is she writing The Love Poems to currently?

I would like to share her insights into her process
as an Earthling poet and what she has learned since.
       There is always the possibility if we are out-of- body
          and I don't come back, I cannot report
              on her continued brilliance.

We both may have moved on. May Out West
       may have become May way out there.
We might not even be interested in poetry anymore.
       She could become Another Animal on Jupiter
          maybe The Centaur
              dwelling in a gaseous Nature.
       I could return to the Pleiades
          to prepare for a mission to the Dal universe.

Like May I believe in "perpetual worlds
       with, upon, above the world."
So, if I am to bring back some of her wisdom to Earth...
       In Other Words, I'd better devise a plan.
          I am not getting any younger
              and could be stardust too...soon.
                 I may already be too late.

What Do I Want to Know?

Thinking is more interesting than knowing, but less interesting than looking. Goethe

A part of me does not want to know.
I enjoy the quizzical thinking quest.
I will continue to look–somehow
when I seek mysteries, openness best.
> There is freedom in the resolution
> to remain skeptical about a solution.

I enjoy the quizzical thinking quest.
Viewpoints and queries ever changing.
If I put my curiosity to rest,
ideas and theories–less wide-ranging.
> I don't need to be a know-it-all.
> I prefer unending search all-in-all.

I will continue to look–somehow
finding new media for resources
as globally, connected minds powwow
to confront challenges from many sources.
> I can contribute a willing soul,
> hope to bring light to any role.

When I seek mysteries, openness best
when exploring all aspects of knowledge.
There is just so much I can digest
and so many concepts I can acknowledge.
> Some areas I can't comprehend.
> With fantasies, I can pretend.

There is freedom in the resolution
not to accept anything at first glance.
Check out contribution's attributions.
Take time to give heart and head a chance.
> I tend to remain ambiguous
> until connection appears contiguous.

To remain skeptical about a solution
keeps me flexible, spontaneous,
expands my consciousness distribution,
sloughs off what's extraneous.
> Just what do I want to know?
> Guess I'll tiptoe as I go.

Soul Sparks

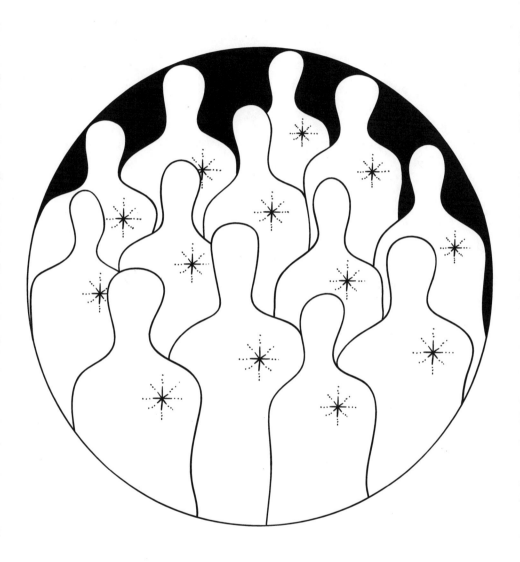

It's about cosmic energy, a little spark of which is inside every individual as the soul.
 - Bharati Mukherjee

Soul-Splitters

The Oversoul is the Soul-splitter
splintering souls for diverse roles.
Each of us is a soul-splinter sitter
living our lives without paroles.
> Peeling away lives from soul-core
> sets us up for one life more.

Splintering souls for diverse roles
does that mean someone assigns
the destiny of all these slivered souls?
We can only hope the purpose aligns.
> What was planned for my birth
> before I whooshed onto Earth?

Each of us is a soul-splinter sitter
at its selected destination.
This time I'm a human critter–
a fragile creature of creation.
> Since I'm here, must puzzle it out,
> affirm imagination, muzzle doubt

Living lives without paroles
until we fulfill why we were sent
avoiding all the folderols
finding ways to consent
> to what is best of life's gifts
> shooing downers for what uplifts?

Peeling away lives from soul-core
infers we live many times in many places.
We must have comeback for an encore.
Perhaps we fell out of our oversoul's graces.
> Whatever the reason I'm perpetually gleaning
> whatever is manifested for deeper meaning.

Sets us up for one life more--
whether we feel ready or not.
We are sent to create and explore.
Personally Earth's a hot spot--
> a place I'm still warming up to.
> I want to be well-done when I'm through.

Radiance

If we move the house of our consciousness built on habit and belief out to the
Unknown, so our new house is the whole universe, amazing things can happen.
We discover radiance everywhere. We begin to see that you and I and all of us, are
patterns stored in Light. Suddenly it's obvious the Dark is what we need to contain
so much Beauty, to hold our wildly, tender, open hearts. Miriam Dyak

All this about moving houses, housekeeping,
patterns of light revealing radiance--
is this what people and Earth are reaping?
It seems we are giving darkness a chance
       to dim beauty and light in our souls.
       It's harder to perform light roles.

Patterns of light revealing radiance
for many of us is just out of sight.
In another dimension images dance
beyond the veil and insight.
       Radiance here has a blurred glow.
       Reserved for shiny realm of halo?

Is this what people and Earth are reaping
or visions of fire, masked from Milky Way?
Layers of pollution, destruction, hatred heaping,
breathing with Gaia, shortening our stay.
       In a dualistic reality curb darkness for light.
       Dark aspects add to people's plight.

It seems we are giving darkness a chance
to win with diminished souls and artificial light.
We must confront each circumstance
where natural, authentic light faces blight.
       If the universe sparks light, is kind,
       we need a better frame of mind.

To dim beauty and light in our souls
gives in to the dark forces.
Gather the parts to connect new wholes,
cooperate and share resources.
       Time to develop strong resilience.
       Time to forge new paths with intelligence.

It's harder to perform light roles
when the news heart-crushes our hopes.
Somehow we have to affirm our light goals.
The light-bringer is the one who love-copes.
       Please, return the radiance to nourish ALL.
       Please, enlighten a new protocol.

Stardusting

Reach high, for stars lie hidden in you. Dream deep, for every dream precedes the goal.   Rabindranath Tagore

Since we are all made from stardust
we all have the right star stuff
to dust off our dreams and thrust
into manifesting our goals-- bluff
      past our challenges and fears,
      ignoring boos for cheers.

We all have the right star stuff
to create our heart's desire.
The path might be rough,
but find some way to inspire.
      Perhaps en route to your goals
      you will have to play many roles.

To dust off our dreams and thrust
our intentions back to the stars,
we might find we must
heals some wounds, bear scars.
      Every innovator and dreamer knows
      we don't always follow where our idea goes.

Into manifesting our goals–bluff
our determination until we see the goal,
but if we lose track, our ears muff
at least we are pursuing spark of soul.
      Reach higher, further to fall
      but when lofty, we heard the call.

Past our challenges and fears
our goals and dreams lure us.
Set straight what's in arrears,
and meet what's before us.
      The only way for dreams to fly
      is to give an ever-onward try.

Ignoring boos for cheers
when you are the different drummer
know it is not what it appears--
perhaps it is them who are dumber.
      Stardusting goals and dreams
      brings on the shining beams.

The Big Questions

While asking about the Big Questions
I have discovered diverse suggestions.

Apparently this life time I came to learn and play
in Earth School and to find my own way?

Creativity is more important than knowledge?
Love can heal and enlighten, many acknowledge?

Science and spirituality harangue
about singularity or The Big Bang?

Then there is what came before
and what essence is at the core?

If we do have the divine within
why does there have to be sin?

Why have evil to know good?
Why not let us act as we should?

Brain delays and becoming mentally ill
give us more complications still?

Throw in wars and addictions
causing pain and afflictions?

Why all the isms that separate us?
Negativism and criticism berate us?

Polarities and dualities increase
reducing harmony and peace?

If we actually all are connected
it's about time we intersected?

Why do we have to rely on hope
when we face situations and can't cope?

How many gods (or not) do people need
to receive guidance and get what they need?

Are there are no accidents or coincidence?
Either way we reap the consequence?

Do we create a life chart before we arrive?
Who guides it? How does our purpose survive?

Who plants ideas in our mind and heart?
How much does our input play a part?

How much of our choices do we control?
Do we get judged? Who is on patrol?

Geniuses claim access to other dimensions.
Why do only some of us have these ascensions?

Can we have diversity with respect?
Enough abundance without neglect?

When we confront challenges highly demanding,
how can we succeed without more understanding?

Why is Earth's reality so harsh, so inequitable,
causing so much suffering, getting less sustainable?

Must we smother, burn to a crisp due to climate change?
Must change bring chaos to create a new interchange?

When was the beginning of sentience? Will we learn?
Blighted evolutions? Creators enhance or spurn?

Have we lost to darkness? Can we reclaim light?
Are we an intelligent species? Can we alter our plight?

Gaia has her own ways to shake up the Earth.
She will persevere as she warms her hearth?

It is the creatures confused in a cloud of unknowing
who have no idea the direction we're going?

Some say all the answers to our questions are within.
If so we can't seem to find them to our chagrin, win?

If we actually have some free will choice,
Will I finally find contentment, truly rejoice?

Spiritual Guidance

You, as a Divine Soul are just as spiritual as any famous guru, teacher, priest, rabbi, master, and so on. A teacher may be a little further on that path than you. But you can't move forward on your path, just by attaching to a teacher. Sara Wiseman

Sara suggests we are a Divine Soul
on our own to find our role.
We need to look beyond guides and ritual
to discover how to be spiritual.

You have to do the work yourself
not rely on workshops or bookshelf.
You have to have the experience to know
what is the best way for you to grow.

You have to grow into your understanding
with your own awakening and branding.
Will you be a spiritual feeder
or become a spiritual breeder?

Personally I like to ponder
diverse possibilities and wonder
about some blather and whether
if I want my soul to tether.

I'd like to remain spiritually open
and awake when new insights happen.
The Divine Soul concept is a mystery.
Not sure how we connect cosmically.

I don't want to lead or follow
just absorb and allow
my intuition and heart to guide me
with whatever help can abide me.

Momentary Fire

O what is life, if we must hold it thus as wind-blown sparks hold momentary fire? Ada Cambridge

Life as windblown sparks of momentary fire
kind of blows my mind.
Brief hot spots then we expire
does not sound divinely kind.
       Winter winds can be cold.
       Smoldering embers hard to hold.

Kind of blows my mind
life's essence here is so temporary
yet eternally on rewind
so says lofty commentary.
       All is energy. Matter can ignite.
       Our job to handle, stoke it right?

Brief hot spots then we expire.
Un-sparked on a breeze,
do we just waft with desire
or endure a deep freeze.
       Some like it cold, some hot.
       Some try to act, some do not.

Does not sound divinely kind
to shoot life-sparks from the Prime Source
to leave these sparklets to find
life experiences with no recourse.
       Once pushed on your own,
       even the body is on loan.

Winter winds can be cold
frostbite on a soul.
Thawing, you must be bold
with so much beyond your control.
       Fire sparks' warmth is temporary.
       Despite our hopes for the contrary.

Warming embers hard to hold
without protective gloves.
Life's temperatures unfold
with our fears and loves.
       While I still kindle my momentary sparks,
       I wonder with awe as my soul embarks.

Wildfires

Like little wildfires, our temper and enthusiasm spark quickly, burn hot and flash out... Let's get started and boldly go where we have not gone before...Their sparky personality is their gift; their challenge is to learn patience and consistency.

Aries Moon signs and Moon transits in We'moon 2016

During the March 23rd lunar eclipse
we were to look within for the "other",
dance with our projections
join up aesthetically
reflect on our inner glow.

We are to stoke our inner fire,
life-fire burning in our bodies.
We take in energy in increments
so we do not ignite and explode.
Perhaps spontaneous combustion
is just an overload of energy.

Spring is time to renew, reawaken,
nourish our inner fire
and all entities that surround us.
Forest fires, freaky fires, war-fires, wildfires,
in unexpected places inflame.

Depression dampens our fires.
Our creative fires, soul fires
try to bring balance, healing.
Sparks of imagination, compassion,
love sparkles from our hearts.

Heart fires appear to be essential
for light and love expressions.
As we confront darkling spirits
with sparkling aspects, we
need to keep the heart hearth
burning by any means possible,
requiring patience and consistency
not an out of control
or flickering flame.

Inter-Dimensional

I have arrived
I am home
in the here
in the now.
I am solid.
I am free
In the ultimate
I dwell.

Zen Buddhist poem

I have arrived
at age seventy-six
full of hope, curiosity, concern.

I am home
in another realm
just visiting here.

In the here
of my beloved green Oregon
in my rainbow house, I muse.

In the now
of climate and cultural upheaval
negativity weighs darkly.

I am solid
too heavily 3-D,
my thoughts are lighter, more fluid.

I am free
from stagnant beliefs
but my mobility is compromised.

In the ultimate
my life spark explores cosmic possibilities
multiversally to sprinkle love.

I dwell
as a soul-sliver of ALL, seek
creative insight to enhance light.

Passing Through

What an amazing process life is, this flow of atoms through time and space. It's just an eternal sequence of events that take form and then instantly dissolves into the next moment. If you resist this amazing force of life, tension builds within you and gets into your body, mind and spiritual heart....If you're neither pushing life away, nor pulling it toward you, then you are not creating any resistance. Michael Singer

To evolve spiritually to the higher path
we need to learn to live life without
stress, problems, fear or melodrama.

Just what are we doing and feeling?
Did I come here to interact or watch?
Beings called Watchers supposedly do that.

I guess I am resistant to just letting
life happen. My willpower can stop
energy transfer creating tension.

It may be a waste of energy but
when the energies of others impinge
negatively on others– do not intervene?

People may not agree how things should be
and how much they should matter.
Impressions cause us to resist or cling.

If life is a gift of flowing events
from birth to death, then we are to remain open
and expansive to encompass reality.

Problems are to be considered stepping-stones
of our spiritual journey while we spin in space
on a challenging planet—passing through.

Bringing light and clarity to situations could help.
Less resistance would occur in a transformed world.
But until then, I expect a blunder-full, bumpy ride.

The Tao is the Middle

Everything has its extremes, its yin and its yang....The Way is the place in which these forces balance quietly. Michael Singer

The Tao addresses the balance of yin and yang,
the feminine and the masculine, the dark and the light.
Like two extremes of the pendulum
there is yin and yang, expansion and contraction,
nondoing and doing with gradations of the swing.
The middle way is the place where there
is no energy pushing in either direction.

Sounds like androgynous beings
dwelling in twilight, resting
with the only exertion, breathing.
That cannot be right or nothing
much would happen. Change
would occur without our interference,
creativity might not spark
in a sluggish, inactive mind.

In reality the extremists attack
the more moderate middle-of-the-roaders.
Warriors disturb the peaceful folk.
Activists of violence prey
on non-participant victims.
The extremes of love and hate
meet in tolerance...sometimes.
Joy and sorrow dimmed
in dulled ache.
The doers outperform the drugged out.
In the middle of good and evil
could be a bland existence.

The quiescent volcano erupts.
Pristine ocean pollutes to point
living things cannot live.
Air becomes unbreathable.
The pole shifts Earth's balance.
The only constant is change.
Hard to maintain your stance
when things are so off-balance.

The Tao states everything
has its yin and yang,
everything has its own balance point.
When all the balance points are in harmony
woven together, it forms the Tao.
The overall balance equilibrium
moves through time and space.
What we are experiencing now
on Earth does not seem Tao
in middle mode. Are we swinging
high toward the dark side
by unbalanced souls and
unsettling natural forces?

The Way or Tao is the place
where energies are balanced.
Many imbalanced people
are drifting to extremes.
Others struggle to center,
not to be caught up in opposites,
participate in the harmony of balance.

I am supposed to reach a point
where my interest lies in the balance,
not in any personal preference
for how things should be. Then
I should sail through life. Life happens,
but I do not make it happen.
Then why am I here? To be an skimmer?

I came to make a difference,
to assist a shift toward the light.
I'd like to act in a balanced way
but at times I'd like to experience extreme
joy and love, fulfillment of a dream.
Moderation in all things may
not be the way I want to swing.
I'd like to touch my toes
to the clouds of unknowing.

Inner Digging

Theories about raising your vibration
by looking within, to discover
who you are meant to be, to know
the secrets encoded in our DNA,
means a lot of introspection,
mysteriously finding the tools to dig.

If we are multi-dimensional beings
vibing on different planes,
does this mean fine-tuning our instrument
to play in different bands?
Maybe we are out of tune
with the cosmic high vibe tribe.

In days of doubt, I ponder whether
to conjure a spade or steam shovel
or tunnel drill to my core. If all is energy,
maybe my wiring would electrocute me.
Is my Earth consciousness disconnected
from cosmic subconscious or superconscious?

Just how do these systems work?
Can I get help with the digging from guides,
in other realms with greater wisdom
and techniques for getting around the cosmos?
Some believe in angels and guides.
I sure hope they are around and not wishful thinking.

I have read about and sought advice
about activation of my inner frequency.
If we are soul-splinters reporting to The Source,
perhaps my Earth splinter is underperforming
and my oversoul is compensating with other splinters.
Maybe I am not meant to know this life time.

When inklings and synchronicities reveal
possibilities for thought and manifestation,
connections to All seem hooked up.
Must I dig deep within or open to the flow,
to get the gist of meaning and direction?
Catch the wave, enhance the vibe, magically?

Satsang

South Asian Sanskrit term meaning a spiritual discourse or sacred gathering,
being in the company of truth or the good with a guru or spiritual students.

Satsang appears a good spiritual suggestion
where a guru speaks about truth,
followed by answering questions.
Like penitent in a confession booth?
      Gathering together to discuss,
      sharing most things is good for us.

Where a guru speaks about truth
is not my spiritual tradition.
Don't want to appear uncouth
but I am not seeking permission.
      But I'd like to discuss truth any time.
      We all seek to know the sublime.

Followed by answering questions?
Sounds like a chance to get clarity,
to mull new tidbits for digestion,
to know with increasing alacrity
      ways truth opens heart and quiets mind.
      Calm the mind. Don't let heart bind.

Like a penitent in a confession booth
can you connect in your computer cube?
Sansang via Internet, Skype, text truth,
teleseminar, catch videos on Youtube?
      Visual or audio forms of media--
      you can be tele-prompting your idea.

Gathering together to discuss
does not have to be in person.
We are all connected–all of us.
With technology do links worsen?
      Sitting cross-legged or on a chair,
      in direct contact, will I be more aware?

Sharing most things is good for us
if done with light-filled spirit.
Satsang concept can open an omnibus
of what we think and intuit.
      I enjoy good company shooting the breeze
      as long as I am not on my knees.

Seeking Spiritual Truths

Perhaps I've become spiritually lazy
not seeking religious or ritual paths.
The abstractness drives me crazy
with division on aftermaths.
       Some texts are very complex.
       I wonder what texts are next?

Not seeking religious or ritual paths
with some Ascended Master at the helm.
Seeking peace from earthly wrath
and guidance from cosmic realm
       from beings, more advanced celestials
       than lower-vibed, backward terrestrials.

The abstractness drives me crazy.
Number of lives needed for enlightenment,
like plucking petals from a daisy
until the core is reached-- fulfillment
       of being one with creation,
       perhaps free of sensation.

With division on aftermaths
of how we live and where we go,
we get cleansed in cosmic baths
sharing what we've come to know.
       I do think there is some plan
       Are we under some ban?

Some texts are very complex
Interpretations are cobbled.
Which translation's best or can vex
those steadied, others still wobbled.
       Consciousness drifts within
       probably from cosmic kin.

I wonder what texts are next.
New Age seems very trendy now.
Still I remain perplexed.
Still without true know-how.
       This starduster aware of Earth
       seeks for my cosmic berth.

Perceptions on Creation

Some religions proclaim a loving God set things in motion.
Some people believe they can count on this God to protect them,
perceive a fatherly figure on a throne. Others–no God.

Some have doubts about understanding how everything began.
Maybe a spark of energy exploded? Whatever the cosmic designer,
they do not claim to know the answers. Maybe there have been
many?

Or creation never gives commands or demands worship
because it is an ego-less, non-judgmental, spiritual force.
Where do you pass the buck to? Actually free will?

Science and spirituality are bridging to find new answers,
insights each discipline can contribute. Is there some
eternal knowledge which guides growth of universe, multiverse?

Patterns for the ways cosmic forces and life forms must evolve?
Can we develop the spirit, access codes, and consciousness to know?
The origins of the universe, life forms, remain a cosmic guess.

It is fun to imagine possible scenarios. Big bang, bubble pop,
collision of branes, energy expansion, new cosmic experiments
devised to enhance life, explore multiple consciousness.

After much contemplation, I can accept ambiguity.
Perhaps we are entering a new age with new ways of thinking.
I am open to diverse viewpoints, anticipating new discoveries.

Getting a Handle on It

"God doesn't give you more than you can handle," say
faith pundits with pompous assurance.
Does the atheist feel that way?
Would an agnostic ask for insurance?
>The concept of God is viewed from many perspectives,
>from a great variety of divinity detectives.

Faith pundits with pompous assurance
portray God as doing challenges for purpose
of growing spiritually, testing our endurance,
but what is the meaning of all of this
>struggle for light through dark pain
>only to face more hurdles again?

Does an atheist feel that way?
Answer questions perhaps by science,
explore electrical and genetic DNA?
Rely more on reason and self-reliance?
>Open to our origins and possible solutions
>without the dogmas of hierarchical resolutions?

Would an agnostic ask for insurance,
proof before skepticism becomes belief?
What would be the defining occurrence
which would bring some meaningful relief?
>Some go through life without a God
>feeling some believers are God-trod.

The concept of God is viewed from many perspectives,
arguing the extent divinity intrudes in our lives.
Hands-off or hands-on become human directives.
Still their free will or chosen spirituality thrives.
>Why would a God burden us to the limit?
>Is this a way to get light-bearers to commit?

From a great variety of divinity detectives,
conceiving dimensions of other realms
not playing Earth games, or retrospectives
with or without rules, diverse helms,
>I am left with a sense of wonder
>and a lot to handle and ponder.

Cracking the Ideal Egg

Life for her has no ritual.
She would break an ideal like an egg for the winged thing at the core. Lola Ridge

A life without ritual could be so freeing...
riding waves in a boat with no anchor...
getting beyond the veil and seeing...
living with love without rancor....
   Giving life to winged things in an egg
   lets the ideal inside fly...unpeg.

Riding waves in a boat with no anchor
could mean no harbor, no grounding,
drifting alone in one's own creation, no shore,
facing storms alone, heart pounding.
   Since we all connect,
   this is the ride few select.

Getting beyond the veil and seeing
more of what the cosmos conceals
is like a virgin bride, curious being
waiting for what life reveals.
   Pull the curtains, start the show
   after any ritual, go with the flow.

Living with love without rancor
would be ideal, but in this world
many lips carried a canker
from which other wounds unfurled.
   Break an egg for most folk
   will mean no chick, but a yolk.

Giving life to winged things in a egg...
a cosmic egg, earthly egg, egg of idea...
encouraging flight for an extended leg
could release a merkaba.
   Ritual can have its place
   if higher consciousness keeps pace...

lets the ideal inside fly...unpeg.
Winged ones let the light escape.
To release higher vibes, I'd beg.
What loftier calling could I agape?
   What ritual would I follow?
   What flight would All allow?

43

Hopeful Horizons

No caste systems or social positions on these planets nor do they recognize any
on other planets that they visit...spiritual masters held in great reverence. God
is ALL and All is God—irrespective of planet, color, race or creed or position.
Such philosophies, which form the basis of all their actions, have rid the planet
forever of ignorance, fear, want, war, disease and political snake-bite-snake
methods so "enjoyed" by backward terrestrials.

Dr. George King   The Aetherius Society

While roaming the Internet in the hope
of making new cosmic connections,
I learned the Aetherius Society's scope,
what they suggest from their reflections.
>   I like the cooperative, compassionate outlook.
>   Appreciate the equality, peaceful stance they took.

Of making new cosmic connections,
I make repeated attempts
Still discovering diverse selections,
keeping an attitude which exempts
>   me from taking a committed stance
>   based on arrogance or ignorance.

I learned the Aetherius Society's scope,
from three Ascended Masters' transmissions:
Aetherius, Mars Sector 6, Jesus tropes
revealing startling cosmic transitions.
>   12 Blessings and 9 Freedoms guide
>   humans from the Other Side.

What they suggest from their reflections,
in each of us beats a spark.
ALL are part of cosmic connections,
light is preferred to being in the dark.
>   Cosmic transmissions reveal a plan
>   to elevate within the cosmic clan.

I like the cooperative, compassionate outlook.
Spiritual welfare offered to all in need.
We could look beyond any holy book
bring a hopeful horizon with increased speed.
       I concur with the group's intentions.
       I willingly explore other dimensions.

Appreciate the equality, peaceful stance they took,
for any belief system can have this at the core.
Science and spirituality, heart and mind can brook--
share information to advance us evermore.
       We have many paths to ponder
       in this wonderful universe out yonder.

Spiritual Evolution

Spiritual advancement is all about service... Spiritual evolution onwards and upwards until greater heights of awareness and service until total absorption into the Divine Source from which we all came in the beginning.
Dr. George King

From some diaspora of soul-splinters,
sparks of consciousness and existence
splattered all over the cosmos.
Some speculate from these experiences
in many forms in many places
after millions of lives of spiritual evolution
each essence returns home to The Source.

One system of advancement
is called the Nine Freedoms.
Some of the guideposts suggested are:

1. Bravery. Fear holds us back.
2. Love. A natural energy greater than mind.
3. Service. Love in practical action.
4. Enlightenment. High intuition.

5. Cosmic consciousness: Mighty heights
    unlimited, unbounded by mind. Higher realms
    of intuition through space where time
    stands quite still, non-existent, immobile.

6. Ascension. Freedom from "wheel of rebirth".
    Ascended Masters help suffering humanity.

7. Interplanetary Existence. Higher material planes
    of respective planets. Move from one plane to another.

8. Saturnian Existence. Saturn has higher frequency
    of vibration than this physical plane, the most advanced
    system in this solar system. Cosmic avatar:
    Sri Krishna came from here with Bhagavad Gita.

9. Solar Existence: Intelligence becomes part
    of the mighty sun itself. State so advanced
    its beyond our comprehension. A state so distant
    it is millions upon millions of lives away.

Quite a long journey. Guess where we each are ?
If we have multidimensional lives
we could be at differing levels.
Based on which soul-splinter gets there first?
Do we have to wait until all splinters arrive?
It at least offers a warm goal line,
a variety of experiences along the way.

Currently I supposedly have 14 simultaneous lives.
Only the one on Earth that I am aware of,
the others elsewhere in the cosmos.
Supposedly I do leave my body at night,
travel in a starship to meet with cosmic chums
and dream in other dimensions
to fulfill other cosmic obligations.

Of the Earth life, there are times
I do not achieve the first freedom.
I wobble in and out of one-three.
Above that would be the higher self
I am not aware of at this time.

According to more intuitive minds,
I do see my celestial son Kip.
On my cosmic trips, we crossed starships
wave and throw kisses.
Intuitives have relayed messages
and I have received energy from him,
once from Aldebaran.
Now apparently he is a sun ray
empowering the Earth.
The sun is the embodiment of service,
giving light and life to the whole solar system.

Many spiritual traditions are based on the sun
and Great Central Sun. But I think beyond
our Milky Way to the unfathomable number
of planets, dimensions, stars, suns, moons.
There must be other Creators shooting sparks
to fill the expanding voids with life.
One central bureaucracy sparkling
unimaginable numbers of soul-splinters–
oh the rigamarole and protocols!
When I think of my oversoul keeping tabs
on my soul-splinters in just this cycle...
my brain and "little brain" of my heart
can just hope energy and consciousness are eternal,
energize with a piece of dark chocolate
and visualize light napping on the couch.

The Four Agreements

Don Miquel Ruiz

The first agreement is to be impeccable
with your word.
This request would be acceptable
especially when heard.

Then don't take things personally.
You are only responsible for you.
Don't absorb negative energy.
What you think is you, you do.

Don't make assumptions.
Ideas might be just a guess.
Take care with presumptions.
You could cause a big mess.

Always do your best.
With some folks that's not a lot.
Many times we fail the test,
have to deal with what we've got.

These agreements in your mind
work best when they connect to heart.
If you dig deeper you might find,
you could agree to take part.

But to me this is an abstraction.
If we are to bode well
we need imagination in action
as far as I can tell.

Redundancies

It's not for me–religion. It seems a redundancy for a poet. May Swenson

Religion seems composed of constricting rules
        like poets endured before free verse.
Religions formed constructs for sinners and fools.
        Unlike poets who prefer things terse,
religion reinforces hierarchies, inequities.
        Poets create anarchies, liberties.

Like poets endured before free verse
        religious folk followed the norms
Poets want to dispute and converse.
        Religious folk stick to "true" forms.
Poets chafe at restriction want to be free.
        Religious folk conform piously.

Religions formed constructs for sinners or fools,
        poets tolerate more diversity.
Religions contain, consensus pools
        poets live and write about adversity.
Poets create their own lines.
        Religions seek what confines.

Unlike poets who like things terse,
        religions compose tomes to obey.
Poets remain open, less prone to curse
        like religions toward those not on their way.
Poets rely on subconscious and instinct,
        don't rely on religions to say how to think.

Religion reinforces hierarchies, inequities
        poets try reach out to all.
Wholly empowered elites cause difficulties.
        Poets explore a freer protocol.
Religions compel a god-fearing kind.
        Poets release thoughts that bind.

Poets create anarchies, liberties.
        Religions think people need patrols.
Poets inspire with luminosities.
        Religions refuse to release controls.
Poets are liberators, inciters of insight.
        Religions persecute, fight for their right.

Opening the Third Eye Chakra

Who knew the pineal gland connected
physical and spiritual worlds, psychic powers?
The third eye chakra links space and time.
Ten minutes a day can open new worlds.

In the morning get comfortable,
place hands on lap, breathe from diaphragm,
inhale and exhale om for ten minutes.
Lighting a candle can help.

The third eye or brow chakra
is considered the seat of the soul,
awakening the eye of Horus.
Five signs indicate third eye opening.

I think I should know what to expect
if I am going to open up to the cosmos.
First my senses will heighten.
My frequency and consciousness will raise.

I could become clairaudient, clairsentient,
clairvoyant, become an intuitive empath,
feel what others are going through.
But I must learn to protect my energies.

Then I go beyond believing to knowing.
I will want to know more, hunger
for more knowledge and information.
I will question reality and belief systems.

I will find power inside myself,
discover meaningful coincidences,
know there are no accidents
and all is held together by mathematical design.
I need to align my energy and awareness
for synthesis, ending dualities.
When I change vibration frequencies
I will realize why things happen.

Another sign is I become health conscious
eating to live instead of living to eat.
Put the best fuel in my tank- no GMO
less sugar, more leafy greens. Coconut water.

Basically realize body, mind and spirit
are connected and if I want to function
at my best, better gravitate toward
a less dark chocolate appetite.

It will be clear the interconnectedness
of all things. Appreciate all life forms.
Become a contributor to uplift the planet.
The time to do this is now.

Apparently the veil is being lifted.
What we know is being questioned.
New horizons are appearing.
Wisdom will set us free.

Opening the third eye more than
a blink or a wink sounds intriguing.
I am poor at meditation, but want
to raise my consciousness and frequency.

I have an inkling of such concepts
and practices. My third eye dwells
in a fat head. Stubbornly I resist
exposing my free will injudiciously.

When my cosmic confidence is bolstered
by my other investigations, then
I might trust myself to open my third eye,
risk getting it blackened for the radiance of light.

Connections

The current buzz is we are all connected--
branches on one family tree.
We can get our DNA tested to know
how we connected over time.

People search for their geneology--
sometimes little more than names
dates, and places they lived. Sometimes
records give a hint to how they existed.

With past life regression you can see
soul patterns., various roles and destinations
like a movie, witnessing your past,
guiding your current karmic challenges.

Multidimensional, simultaneous lives
also inform this earthly incarnation.
Your soul-splinters are also learning
to add to cosmic libraries, Akashic records.

If true, what does the universe do
with all these experiences,
struggles with existences for what?
To discover meaning and purpose for who?

Will all my soul-expressions end up
in dusty archives on a shelf,
a computer byte in a cosmic computer,
a fading holographic image? Time travel peeks?

Do we have the choice of best options
for ourselves and associates?
In just this life, who will play Earth games
with you and where have these players played?

I would want to choose positive, peaceful creations
and fair, equitable interactions. Hopefully
my higher self is guided by higher entities
so I can manifest light, love, harmony.

But if earthly consciousness is an illusion
and we have many games to play to evolve,
we seem on shaky ground to be grounded–
especially when we have ethereal dreams.

DNA Activation

If my DNA is experiencing mutations
to activate to a higher vibration
and higher consciousness
I need to be aware of certain symptoms:

Vertigo, dizziness, muscle pains, imbalance,
feeling drunk, ear ringing, jaws stick, grind teeth,
lower back and neck pain, sore arms,
anxiety, panic attacks, heart palpitations.

Flu-like symptoms nobody can diagnose.
Can't get words together when you speak.
Experience tongue-twisters, just don't feel good
and no one can give you the answers why.

Some pundits claim the sun is doing it.
You will be hungry for sweets or not
feel like eating. Try small fruit and veggie shakes.
Anxiety comes with solar flares.

You can't stand crowds, watch news on TV,
get sick from negativity. You are not alone
millions suffer with you–unless you are a child
who was activated before birth.

So what can one do? Sun brings more
than sunburn and cancer. Relax.
Go for walks, listen to music, work in the garden.
Surround yourself with positive people.

We can pamper ourselves. No diets.
Eat cookies and ice cream if we want.
Protect yourself from anxiety and people
who don't feel good because of it.

Send light and compassion. People are afraid.
Go homeopathic with pills to relax--
Valarian and St. John's wart.
Do stretching and yoga. Limber up.

Our muscles tense. We misalign spine.
Stomach troubles. So eat light portions,
drink lots of water and veggie juice, meditate
just relax, laugh, enjoy your unique dreams.

This DNA activation though somewhat troublesome
perhaps could enhance our future prospects.
I've experienced symptoms, tried remedies.
Someday we begin to see sparkles of light.

Dreams of Spirit Guides

We all could use a little support
from other realms. Some spirit guides
could be angels, ascended masters, light orb,
earth and mystic guides, spiritual teachers,
lanky wise guides, beautiful women in gowns,
monks, extraterrestrials, even fairies or leprechauns.

Guides manifest in ways we can understand--
tiny or tall, with humor, peacefully--
a multidimensional friend. Spirit guides
present themselves to appeal to our inner child
and make us wiser. Powerful shape-shifters
they to cater to our preferences.

Various cultures perceive beings
watching over each person from birth--
a guardian to help us through this incarnation.
I'm fascinated by fairies and angels.
I am not opposed to benign cosmic companions.
I wonder if we get to pick before we show up?

I am not gifted with special perceptual gifts.
For me it a matter of hope I get some help.
I tend to believe when I fell backward
down an up elevator, I was rescued
by an angel in a Hawaiian shirt who
mysteriously disappeared before learning his name.

Intuitives say we are all surrounded by several angels,
spirit guides of some kind. Religions tend
to support what science has not detected.
I am comfortable with hope and fantasy,
driven by an instinct for the supernatural,
dreaming I have access to the guidance I need.

Sharpen Your Love in the Service of Myth.

Rita Dove

In Mythic times love goddesses romped through the forest
bosoms bouncing, Rubenesque bellies dancing,
entrancing a handsome Adonis or a Narcissus
sharpening his self image in a mirrored pool.
Some goddesses are seduced by a swan.

Myths create expectations of love
feathery fantasies sharpened by reality.
Love is not served by illusion.
Unconditional love has few role models
in surreal or real settings.

Long-tresses curl over voluminous curves,
six-pack men stand studily.
How often are lovers topless in public?
Selfies are taken inside, go to social media,
not posing in parks or on street corners.

Sharpening love requires clarity,
removing the fog of infatuation.
Sharp observation not words.
Still, a little mythic quality enhances enchantment.
...at least for a little while.

Love can be a dagger to the heart.
Think Romeo and Juliet.
Think all of the tragic, deluded heroines.
Sometimes we just aren't sharp
when it comes to love.

Diamonds

It is as if a large diamond were to be found inside each person. Picture a diamond a foot long. The diamond has a thousand facets, but the facets are covered with dirt and tar. It is the job of the soul to clean each facet until the surface is brilliant and can reflect a rainbow of colors. Brian Weiss

Lugging around a foot-long, tar-encrusted, dirty diamond
inside us seems like a heavy, scummy metaphor.
What cleanser do we use? Environmentally friendly?
Where's the scrub brush? Most effective brand?
Why would our facets need to be marred?
Some say we are created with a clean slate.

If it is the soul's job to scrub off this miasma
so all the facets are shiny and spewing
a spectrum of lights, are there instructions to do so?
If we succeed, supposedly our diamond returns
to pure energy to exist in a rainbow of lights.
The lights possess consciousness and knowledge.
But how do we get there without consciously
knowing what we are doing? Subconscious intervention?

Guess the difference between people
is the number of cleaned facets.
Some might prefer to be mired in darkness.
Others might learn to become more "God-Like"
and seek balance, harmony and inner peace.
Some could have insider insights on how to reduce fear
reach out to others with love, without muddy hearts.

Appears I should cleanse the facets of my soul
until they clear, glisten, reflect.
Yet I am a diamond in the rough
until I am unearthed to be shaped,
until I polish my surfaces.
I remain unclear how to achieve this clarity.

A diamond on my hand sparkles, as an outward
reminder for over 55 years to focus on love.
My soul-diamond has had plenty of time
to clean up my act and show some glow.
Time to find some more effective diamond cleanser
as I seek for solutions through science,
spirituality, art on my cosmic quest to reveal light?

However I am a haphazard house-keeper.
My dim soul-facets await illumination.
Any radiant reflections need more company.
Can I rub off my soul-facets' surfaces to emanate brilliance
as I focus on this earthbound soul-splinter's existence?
Do I have the resources to control my soul's brightness?
As a multi-dimensional being, I hope other places
may have very different metaphorical expressions to ponder.

It would be frabjous to believe we have
innumerable opportunities to become luminous,
to remove the sticky scum and oozy grime from this life.
Perhaps light penetrates life like a laser,
but I wonder why do our facets need
to be tarnished at any stage of life.

I am glad this soul-diamond concept is only a metaphor
for a very murky metaphysical soul challenge--
to sparkle shadowy, messy aspects
so all soul-facets can be lightsome.

Cosmic Sparks

Theories linking spirituality and science
spark speculation on cosmic origins, Earth and human roles.
New theories of Oneness from this new alliance
find physics and metaphysics full of holes,
      revise religions and current physics alas,
      question many laws and beliefs, demote Einstein second class.

Spark speculation on cosmic origins, Earth and human roles,
from the perspective of an Electric Universe,
where we can have contacts instantaneously, bowls
over our concepts of change and brings in a multiverse.
      of instant gratification in zero time,
      a future which is really sublime.

New theories of Oneness from this new alliance
study mer-ka-ba science, explore sacred geometry
probe Birkeland currents, Heartmath reliance
to understand various forms of energy.
      Big, Bang, black holes, dark matter, gravity --so long
      these solutions new investigators won't prolong.

Find physics and metaphysics full of holes
means new understandings will unfold,
requires opening horizons, releasing rigmaroles,
new approaches for the dimensionally bold.
      New wisdom to solve problems and healing
      leaves us stunned, consciousness reeling.

Revise religions and current physics, alas
for a human race who has not understood
how to bring light, who quagmires in a dark morass--
would bring new hope to our galactic neighborhood.
      Earth suffers from our unsustainable stewardship,
      our dim sentience, low vibe, misguided worship.

Question many laws and beliefs, demote Einstein second class--
new innovators, geniuses are moving us forward.
Can we make a dimensional shift with a critical mass?
Discover new insights to propel us onward?
      If we are all energetically connected to All,
      perhaps humanity will answer the cosmic call.

Enlightenment Awareness

Do not think you will necessarily be aware of your own enlightenment. Buddha

Even if you are paying attention
you might still not be aware.
Your enlightenment's retention,
your consciousness might not share.
> Not knowing is a bit of a relief.
> Less commanding than belief.

You might still not be aware
of your spiritual attainment,
even though you were heading there,
your soul's not ready for arraignment.
> Even if you meditate,
> your challenges agitate.

Your enlightenment's retention
may be cloudy, lack clarity.--
So despite your very best intention,
you're not moving with alacrity.
> Yet you might find the contrary.
> Your enlightenment might be alary.

Your consciousness might not share
your sub-or-super consciousness.
Enlightenment could be hidden anywhere
taming its rambunctiousness,
> while we seek harmony and peace,
> for pain and suffering to release.

Not knowing is a relief.
We are each responsible for our soul.
We'll experience a lot of grief
trying to be spiritually whole.
> Maybe we have made progress
> toward the Enlightened Congress?

Less commanding than belief
is the freedom to explore
routes to enlightenment, a chief
goal gurus and guides implore.
> So whether I uplift of not,
> maybe I did and then forgot?

Dancing Sparks

We need only stay close. In time, sparks will fly. J. Cole

Unexpected Light

While resting beneath a sun-streaming window
I spied a white orb dancing on the wall.
I protected my face from sun to disavow
any return of skin cancer et al.
   But the orb began to dance.
   The glowing spot continued to entrance.

I spied a white orb dancing on the wall
and found the surface of my watch the cause.
When I moved my hand quickly, light would waterfall,
swish swiftly dot-to-dot like comet, pause
   on bureau--an angel collection to spotlight.
   If glass–a sparkle gleams with clear delight.

I protected my face from sun to disavow
more surgical gouging of my nose.
Sun on age-spotted hands, I allow
though could become cancery, I suppose.
   But I was fascinated by light-dots,
   played like shadow puppet hand with light-spots.

Any return of skin cancer et al
was not my focus as I played.
Just belly-breathing bounced light to enthrall.
All thoughts of my rising were delayed.
   Sunlight rainbowed-white across the room
   bringing objects into bright bloom.

But the orb began to dance
only when I moved my hand.
Still reclined I took a chance
to perform light-dances on command.
   No way I would want to nap
   when I could play with a wrist snap.

The glowing spot continued to entrance.
I tried to use my clogged diamond ring.
I tooth-picked gunk from facets to enhance
the glistening glory it could bring.
   But when I stood, walked away from sun
   my hand darkled, light-dancing done.

Let Go and Dance

Let go and you're a dancer on the wind. Carolyn Myers

Leaf-ish I face the brisk autumnal wind
not the whirlwind of wildfires
still out of control to the south.
I'm not a whirling dervish.

My mind swirls, though my body can't.
I want to let go of anxiety
twirling around inside me
but my stiff legs keep me a wallflower.

If I could let go and dance
freely moving on earth or stage,
I'd dazzle the dance floor,
flinging limbs to the beat of my heart.

Dancers

Life is the dance and we are the dancers. Eckhart Tolle

Earth dances have diverse music, tempos and songs.
We take dance lessons throughout our life spans.
We learn the skills where each step belongs.
We hope to express our cosmic plans.
　　　　Sometimes I tiptoe, sometimes I stomp.
　　　　Sometimes I pirouette, sometimes I romp.

We take dance lessons throughout our life spans,
look for creative inspiration inwardly and out.
Our audience is not always our biggest fans.
We struggle to know what the dance is about.
　　　　Sometimes I partner, sometimes I solo.
　　　　Sometimes I stumble, sometimes systems all go.

We learn the skills where each step belongs.
Intuitively we seek to choreograph our part.
In this earthly ensemble as the dance prolongs,
we wait for true understanding to start.
　　　　Sometimes being a terpsichorean is hard.
　　　　Sometimes I wear sweats or a leotard.

We hope to express our cosmic plans
through multiversal dances in 3D
connected to other Earthling also-rans
in Prime Source's eternal creativity.
　　　　Sometimes a new dance style's created.
　　　　Sometimes this dance is not appreciated.

Sometimes I tiptoe, sometimes I stomp
as the stages change, spotlight varies.
I prefer simplicity to complex pomp
as I twirl and whirl with contemporaries.
　　　　Sometimes I'm lyrical or prefer hip-hop.
　　　　Sometimes I'm classical or enjoy be-bop.

Sometimes I pirouette, sometimes I romp.
At times I'm exhausted, at times I'm inspired.
Sometimes I stretch, sometimes I tromp,
but I persevere beyond when I'm tired
　　　　for this dance time is where I'm at now
　　　　and I'll dance until I drop...somehow.

Love Dancers

Love is a dance, high energy and passion...what if you could see love in the air, like color? Derek Hough

Speckles of sunrise, swashes of sunset?
What colors? Who chooses? Any stereotypes?
Would each of us exude our colorful love-vibes
and sprinkle the sky with rainbows of love particles?

Would we emit love colors for special occasions
like engagements, weddings, anniversaries?
Would we honor loved ones with their special color
like purple splashes in honor of Prince?

These love-bits could dance to the rhythms
of their hearts, twirls and swirls of colors,
Love vortexes, helixes, jigs, clogs, waltz.
Hot Latin dances– auras ablaze with love-fire.

With all this colorful love dancing around us
we could get caught up in the spirals,
unloved ones could catch love like a virus.
Would the love dancers be luminous?

Could colorful love dancers sustain the energy,
or get blown away and diffused?
Would we get caught up being light dancers
and forget more solid expressions?

It could all be so ethereal, mystical
create a color fog, blurring vision.
But what a light-hearted spirit, so at least
a little while to sparkle a darkled world!

Dancing Mike

There's no right or wrong way to dance.   Mike Ambrosius

When I dance I don't think
about anything at all.
I don't think about money, abuse,
epilepsy, parenting my son Toron.
When I dance I don't think
about the past or future.
        I just do it.

        Dance is about freedom just to be.
        Dance without expectation and be free.

Wet,
dry
I dance
around town,
solo or partnered,
being myself body and soul.

        Dance is about freedom just to be.
        Dance without expectation and be free.

My adoptive Grandma in foster care
        taught me to dance when I was ten.
Five years ago I started to be free.
        In a concrete garden I dance again.

There's some things in life
        you're never going to get past.
I have to deal, but don't have to dwell.
        I'm a dance enthusiast.

Looking for something to do without money,
        music from a nightclub lured me in.
But though shunned, insulted, assaulted,
        some pay to see my dance begin.

I dance on sidewalks and streets.
        Some places I've become a fixture.
I've performed at benefits and clubs.
        My reception has been a mixture.

In some people I've caused fear,
    being free-spirited is a threat.
Some want to pay me to stop,
    but I haven't accepted those payments yet.

Though standing ovations are nice,
    I am not looking for validation.
At 44 I do splits, dance impromptu.
    I dance through a difficult situation.

    Dance is about freedom just to be.
    Dance without expectation and be free.

To dance
requires me
to be wiry and trim.
I fling my long hair like oak limbs.
My tree of creativity
includes drawing, poetry, martial arts.
Favorite dance is western swing,
stay limber so free
to dance.

    Dance is about freedom just to be.
    Dance without expectation and be free.

My dance
does not
please some. They think
I'm nuts,
but I find space
by chance.

Like a
spring
daffodil,
rainbow, I bloom,
bring light, pop, lock
my dance.

    Dance is about freedom just to be.
    Dance without expectation and be free.

Seeking Heartfelt Things

The best and most beautiful things in the world cannot be seen or even touched-
they must be felt with the heart.   Helen Keller

What if my senses didn't make sense of the world,
a deaf and blind dancer flailing,
none of my limited input unfurled
from inhaling and exhaling.
> When I return to my essence
> maybe then all will make sense.

A deaf and blind dancer flailing
still can experience a loving touch.
I follow with my heart, trailing
any manifestation. Insomuch
> as my heart resonates,
> my soul celebrates.

None of my limited input unfurled
even when senses supposedly function.
Oh to create a beautiful world
at this critical planetary junction.
> My dancing days are restricted,
> but my heart need not be constricted.

From my inhaling and exhaling
the breathe of spirit lives
with hope of love prevailing.
I ponder just what gives.
> I can't absorb such complexity
> without profound perplexity.

When I return to my essence
in a lighter, brighter place
will I laugh at earthly pretense,
the hubris of the human race.
> My comfort lies knowing I'm not alone.
> Heart pounding, I am cosmically prone.

Maybe then all will make sense
when my equipment is eliminated,
when I rid myself of nonsense
and consciousness will be illuminated.
> When formless, stardust from afar
> all dances no matter what we are.

Cosmic Dance

> *I am made up of stardust...once a piece of a star shining in the heavens. I am part of a vast and marvelous dance that goes on unceasingly in every moment of the most minute particles of the universe. Each of us is a dancer in this cosmic dance. Few people are aware of this Dance even though everyone and everything in our universe is part of the dance.   Joyce Rupp*

Just think, I am a conglomeration of dancing molecules
glomming into bone and tissue to dance--
an ensemble of stardust!

How does energy compact to densely dance
on a heavy planet after drifting unseen
sparkly and darkly through this universe?

This clunky dancer with limp limbs,
less-than-lithe body, enjoys dance
in any of its forms and formless.

The Creator Choreographer, Multiversal Terpsichore
puts on a frabjous show wherever performed,
an energetic dance electrifying the cosmos.

There is love-oriented dance between energies
of unconditional love and unceasing light.
Turn on the music and get me in the mood to dance.

Wu Li Dancers

The dance of subatomic particles never ends and it is never the same. Gary Zukav

If the only constant is change
and everything is energy,
dancing is eternal.

If "Wu" means "matter" or "energy"
and "Li" means "universal order"
or "universal law", the cosmos dances.

Al Huang condensed the multiple
meanings of Wu Li in Chinese:
> Patterns of Organic Energy
> My Way
> Nonsense
> I Clutch My Ideas
> Enlightenment

A Wu Li Master teaches essence
and dances with a student until
perception is expanded.

In explaining the world
Wu Li Masters know
they are only dancing with it.

Huang feels "Every lesson is the first lesson
and every time we dance,
we do it for the first time."

Every time we use our imagination
we dance. It is always new, personal
and alive. You experiment.

Zukav says Wu Li Masters dance in midst of all--
this way and that, sometimes with heavy beat,
sometimes with light and grace, flowing freely.

They become part of the dance
and the dance becomes them. Don't confuse
the type of dance with fact they are dancing.

Dance the light fantastic
seems a good motto. Dance
with subatomic particles...with ALL.

Ehanamani's Sundance Vision Quest

On Ehanamani's vision quest,
the Lakota Sundance Chief
saw we were all related
and how we are connected to the Pleiades.

The head of the white buffalo constellation
holds the seven stars of the Pleiades
the original home of the spirits who said
we have lost telepathy and how to light up a room.

In a starship he witnessed
masters of time, laws of light and thought.
We need these abilities
to help humanity survive.

Earth has way portals, is an exchange center.
Master geneticists tweaked various species,
in this living cosmic library of beauty,
stored in frequencies and genetics.

Light is information and dark is no information.
After galactic conflicts Earth became
a place of duality and uninformed free will.
We are left with a limited frequency band.

When our DNA was rearranged to a two-stand
double helix, the rest were unplugged
to keep the elites in power. Pleiadeans
came back to help to raise our frequency.

We are kept in control by emotional trauma.
Part human, part reptilian Lizzies
feed on emotions. We should open
our ancient Horus eyes and see our connectedness.

We can raise the feelings inside of us
to a sense of knowing, divine ecstasy.
We are part of a divine plan. We hold
the history of the universe inside us.

73

Our DNA is evolving to 12 helixes, 12 vortexes
and chakras. We can become super beings.
We can break down the layers that held us down,
become renegades, ambassadors to release fear.

We need to turn up the dial from our low frequency
which sealed off our planet from higher vibes
to receive creative cosmic rays of knowledge
to share to alter the planet.

We are all united—one heart and one body
We are in one small galaxy of billions,
yet we think we are all alone. Wake up.
The Family of Light, not just Pleiadeans have come.

The Family of Light came to assist transition.
They are entities to trigger you,
here on assignment for your own knowing.
They have trained for lifetimes for this mission.

Remember your training. Remember what you know.
Humanity is an experiment of the Prime Creator.
We are to go out and create to bring all things
back to the The Source- stored in cosmic libraries.

Our mission is to librate the dance of self, find your tune.
To what heights can we push our consciousness?
Teams hold frequencies from the Central Sun-
supreme achievers in the multidimensional realm.

Can we become a member of the light team,
soothe and awaken a new species, bring freedom
to evolve back to the planet? Take back power
for a new world order? Rescue enslaved humans?

Ehanamani believes the place is here,
the time is now. Can we join the sundance?
Can we raise consciousness to effect
the entire universe? It is a sparkling light vision.

Labyrinths

This labyrinth symbolizes the spiritual path
to commune with God signified in the center.
Dance and ritual trap evil spirits' wrath.
Meditatively, silently, I slowly enter.
   A circular, meandering journey leads
   one to discover uncovered veiled needs.

To commune with God signified in the center
is not really this mission's intent.
At a writing workshop, I seek muse mentor
to guide a poem with my consent.
   Awkward, I stay inside the spiraling lines
   to see if my imagination aligns.

Dance and ritual trap evil spirits' wrath
according to ancient divine traditions.
Hoping for an enlightened aftermath
I want to make similar creative transitions.
   Will I achieve a contemplative state
   or will I lallygag and arrive too late?

Meditatively, silently I slowly enter
concentrating on footsteps and thought,
followed by another more devout repenter.
Would my effort be all for naught?
   Will I find deep knowledge on my way
   encoded within myself and DNA?

A circular, meandering journey leads
us possibly to higher understanding.
As my aging, achy body pleads
to make it to the end still standing.
   This pattern of sacred geometry
   continues to be a challenge for me.

One to discover uncovered veiled needs
to struggle onward rounding circles to the core.
One falls, gets up, bruises and bleeds,
toward higher realms, cosmic order to explore.
   While this labyrinthian maze sprawls on Earth,
   my physical being seeks a metaphysical berth.

Grounding Sparks

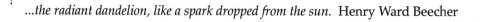

...the radiant dandelion, like a spark dropped from the sun. Henry Ward Beecher

The Count Down

Earth could be home to roughly 1 trillion species and 99.999 percent remain
undiscovered.   Research funded by National Science Foundation's
Dimensions of Biodiversity program

Biologists report Gaia's glut of life forms
to be astoundingly abundant.
Microscopic and non-microscopic norms
to reveal trillions of species are extant.
>   Another example of one-percent power.
>   But 99% masses refuse to cower.

To be astoundingly abundant
means 20,376 samples of fungi, bacteria, archaea.
15,000 samples of mammals resonant
with bird and tree communities area.
>   People are vastly outnumbered.
>   Gaia is seriously encumbered.

Microscopic and non-microscopic norms
need ecological models and rules,
a data base that informs.
So solutions and discoveries pool.
>   Microbial biodiversity is greater than imagined.
>   So many creatures remain undefined.

To reveal trillions of species are extant
required global cooperation.
Datasets from all continents
provided the illumination
>   that people can study other forms of life
>   but it is Gaia who is the midwife.

Another example of one-percent power.
The overwhelming majority is not heard
or wants known, waiting for a force to empower
the needs of Gaia's nervous, hungry herd.
>   Can any group really protect?
>   What is known we tend to neglect.

But 99% masses refuse to cower.
Each entity struggles to survive in a space.
If apocalyse comes, begins to scour,
teeny, tiny micro-bits could win the race.
>   5.6 million known species big and small
>   from more than 35,000 global spots downfall.

Broad-Based Plant Report

Royal Botanical Gardens at Kew Report

Uses of Plants

*Of 391,000 plant species only about 30,000
had documented use for people.*

Cherish plants.
Bloom enchants.
Elegance
source of chants,
resonance.

Food to eat
Fuel: deplete
Worn: replete
Kill: complete
building feat.

Results of Tests

*Of the vascular plants
94 percent have flowers*

Only
plants called
vascular, count.
They
have water tubes.
Mosses,
algae:
none.
Many
cannot adapt,
face extinction,
losses.

Threats to Plants

*Most major plant groups take
10, 20, 30 years for next generation.*

Plants threatened: invasive species,
changing climate, land, diseases.
Extinction for one of five plants.
Limited time. Protests cause rants, interstices.

Generations to reproduce
flowers, pollen. Can gap reduce?
In frigid Svalbard, global seed source
in vault in arctic. Hopeful force: doomsday bank course.

Prediction

Botanists fear
plant decline's near.

Hopeful Scenario

Gradual change
keeps loss less range?

Botanists' Concern

Useful plants prime
for borrowed time.

Uncounted

Mosses, algae—
immunity?

Global Report

Global Warming:
plants give warning.

Interconnected

If plants can thrive,
we may survive.

Farewell to Tulips

Where have all the flowers gone?
One million tulips endangered
by land use changes over time.
The 160 acre-plus farm bought in 1958
sees siblings squabbling
over whether to sell or
keep parent's land for farming.
One brother doesn't want to see
the land developed, but he says
it isn't his choice.

Washington County put 1,190 acres
into the urban growth boundary.
61,000 acres in the County
has been lost to development
in 33 years.

When the land moved from urban reserves
for future development, the clan
reaped significant value added
to their family farm. The brother
is out of time.   Conservation groups
lost their appeal. The land swapped,
locked and legislated into developable
and undevelopable behind closed doors.

In five to ten years the land
will become housing.
One million multi-colored tulips, 26 varieties
planted at this farm will be gone.
150,000 people are expected
to live in Hillsboro by 2040
an increase of 60 percent.
The farm is too close and will
be gobbled up. Too close
to the new Hillsboro airport.

Like many small organic farms
and nurseries, this farm that once
grazed cows will be gone.
Slow moving farm equipment
transits to slow moving urban traffic.

Where have all the flowers gone?
Gone to houses, everyone.
As populations grow, water goes
to drink, not to food and flowers.
Where will we find
wild flowers and tulips nearby?
With climate change
water shortages predicted,
how will we manage our resources?

When will we ever learn?
When will we ever learn?

Life's Extremists

Archaea - domain or kingdom of single-celled microorganisms. These microbes are prokaryotes meaning they have no cell nucleus or any other membrane-bound organelles in their cells.

Archaea are the newest life form domain
discovered in extreme conditions
like thermal vents and hyper-saline water.

Archaea thrive in hot springs, alkaline or acid waters,
in plankton on open seas, rift vents, on ocean bottom,
anoxic mud in marshes, petroleum deposits deep underground.

Archaea create methane in termites,
marine life, the digestive tracts of cows—
assist cow farts and cow-pies.

Archaea like environmental extremes—
places hostile to all other life forms—
a diverse, abundant clade or organisms.

With our fascination with tiny things,
nanotechnology, ever increasing capacity
to see micro and macro—we may find new life forms.

In moon dust, on comets and meteorites
mini-life hitch-hikers from alien worlds,
bring stardust to earth to enhance life.

Life's extremists in human form inflame hot spots.
Terrorists destroy World Heritage sites, kill civilians,
abuse hostages, wire children with suicide bombs.

Perhaps people in the animal life kingdom
will take destructive actions to such extremes
Archaea will inherit the Earth.

Plastic Lovers

Bacteria capable of eating plastic were an inevitability. The tiny cells are
evolutionary dynamos. Philip S. Wenz

Bacteria can clone themselves in 20-30 minutes.
50-75 generations and hundred of millions in 24 hours.
Bacteria swap genes, absorb other genetic material.

Literally quadrillions of opportunities to evolve,
produce enzymes and biochemical pathways
to digest new food sources like plastics.

Microbes feed greedily in the Sargasso Sea
on floating plastic flotsam and jetsam
in one of the oceanic garbage patches.

In China waxworms with bacteria
in their guts thrive on eating Styrofoam
and polyethylene plastic bags.

In Japan bacteria eat scraps of PET
in a bottling plant's waste water, PET
can be found in polyester in majority of synthetic fibers.

In twenty years more plastic bottles than fish in the sea.
More plastic than any other material in landfills.
A bonanza for bacteria. An environmental disaster for us.

The good news bacteria could be a solution
to world's plastic waste problems,
could curb landfill buildup and oceanic pollution.

Genetic engineering could speed their metabolism, refine reproduction.
But bacteria could turn on us and our technology,
expand their tastes and find us appetizing.

They could nibble us naked in our synthetic clothes,
gobble the innards of our cars, cremate computers,
eliminate medical and media equipment.

Scientists found four million mostly unknown species
in a ton of soil. Globally, bacteria called dark matter
of the biological world could be insidious everywhere.

Unseen, they lurk creeping, slithering surfaces
gorging inside and beneath us, infiltrating air?
Bacteria could inherit the Earth.

Tardigrades: Cosmic Climate Changers

Tardigrade made of a hardy grade
of stolen and foreign genes, microanimals
who reside all over the world in the most
extreme climates -- yet survive conditions
fatal to nearly all other known life forms.
Just the size of a period.

They can go without food or water for decades,
when the climate does not suit them,
they go into suspended animation,
to dry out, rehydrate, forage and reproduce
when the conditions are right.
They endure climate changes people might not.

Called "water bears" or "moss piglets",
I wonder if they growl or oink.
Eight plump legs with claws, sucking pharynx
on a roly-poly, soft, segmented body,
they feed on mosses, lichens, algae,
plant cells, small invertebrates.

Tardigrade live in the deep sea trenches, high
in the Himalayas, Antarctic ice, hot springs, beaches
ponds, moss, dunes, dirt, dust, soil, sediment,
polar regions to equator--the only species to survive
outside Earth's atmosphere in cold, open, vacuum
of space, unshielded solar radiation.

These "Sleeping Beauties" revive in petri dishes
after decades, for they switch genes on and off.
They withstand high and low pressure,
repair DNA from radiation. Scientists burn,
starve, squish, freeze, radiate them, but
awakened, they wiggle to life, lay eggs.

Tardigrades are an ancient life form
at least back to the Cambrian period.
They steal genes from other species
like bacteria, plants, fungi and Archaea.
Their ability to shut down their systems
lets them survive climate changes -- almost anywhere.

They can dry themselves out, dust themselves off
start all over again. The most durable organism
discovered, did they arrive by meteorite?
Survive space travel and adjust to landing here?
Would they survive an Earth apocalypse, become hybrids--
"Captain Tardigrade-defender of the Multiverse?"

Slugs

Spring brings slinky slugs
to slime the garden and
even our home's green walls.

They emerge from winter underground
shelter to nibble mostly at night
hide mostly in the day.

This is their time of year.
They dislike winter and summer.
They are ready to munch green.

Conscientious slug-phobes plant
herbs, more sturdy and woody plants
like ferns, bleeding heart, ornamental grasses.

But our garden has their favorites:
strawberries and daffodils. They like lettuce,
salad greens, broccoli, beans—

which we like, but do not grow.
We have slugged slugs with beer tubs,
but we have not attracted predators—

ducks, frogs, ground beetles, snakes
who like slug snacks. More abundant
places might be more appealing to them.

I do not want to go slug-picking,
use salt which damages soil, use
toxic baits, wrap copper bands on pots.

I am sluggish in my approach.
I am content to share and leave
gardening to my husband.

The Ivy League

Far from eastern Ivy League schools
at a western state college
thirty rental goats eat invasive ivy weed
-a new ivy league to acknowledge.

Natural weed eaters, no need for weed whackers,
no clippings, no stash to haul
to compost site, no heavy equipment.
A pesticide alternative. A good deal for all.

Goats love ivy, poison oak, greens,
thistles, blackberries, Scotch broom–
their favorite munch-away, take-in menu.
The campus gave goats ½ acre to groom.

Five pounds a day of ivy provides
fertilizing mulch, paves the way
for native plantings to return.
A goat-herder on call night and day.

A shepherdess keeps herd on task.
Poly-wire netting fences keeps goats in place.
All three-year old males–same size
roommates sharing green rental space.

The grazers become a tourist attraction.
Student and staff paparazzi shoot photos and gawk
as goat-grubbers work a while, stop, rest
contentedly chew their cud from each stalk.

The goats will work the night shift,
but some want to jump the fence, escape.
It's soothing and relaxing to watch the goats,
decreasing stress of campus landscape.

Migratory goats have a tight schedule
serving apartment complexes, vineyards,
garden and schools. Environmentally natural,
goat-gleaners are green-grazing vanguards.

Goats find treasures heavy equipment can't
like boats, irrigation ponds, propane tanks.
On campus they found many bottles.
They chew their livelihood without much thanks.

Shepherdess wants a permanent goat home
preferably with free food like blackberries,
but with her ivy league working full-time
she and rental goats reduce environmental worries.

New Visions for Elephants and Rhinos

Kenya is making a statement that for us ivory is worthless unless it is on our elephants" Kenya's President Uhuru Kenyatta

Stacks of tusks of more than 8,000 elephants
and 343 rhinos slaughtered for their ivory.
Pyres were burned to make the point
they do not have commercial value.

However, selling the ivory would mean
$150 million dollars that could have been used
to develop Kenya and protect wildlife
from international gangs breeching porous borders.

Illegal trade diminished African elephants
from 1.3 million in the 1970's
to only 500,000 today. Central Africa's decline
of forest elephants is two-thirds between 2002-2012.

Gabon's President Ali Bongo Ondimba
wants to put all poachers out of business.
Buyers and foreign traders must be stopped,
if they are to prevent the decline of the species.

Last year, about 1,300 animals were slaughtered
in South Africa due to high demand in China and Vietnam
for their horns. How can we sustain all species
without killing each other, so no longer viable?

80 critically endangered rhinos were shipped
to Australia to prevent extinction. If successful
they will go to Texas and Florida, to establish
"insurance populations" and a diverse gene pool.

When an American dentist killed a lion,
many were outraged and airlines
would not transport trophy heads.
What about not shipping tusks?

In the Jungle Book they had laws--
even times of truce between the animals.
But that is fantasy, though a compelling start.
Yet 11 pyres of ivory tusks, one of rhino--burns.

Litter or Large Ort

Depending on the angle
a black object dropped
on a dirt parking lot
is either a large ort
-part of an eyeglass
or cosmetic case.
Perhaps it's just littered
from a small umbrella casing,
or travel tooth brush container.

From different angles
you can guess it is a
chocolate paper wrapper
from a box of candy
or a tubular covering
for something.

Sitting in the car I watch
a dog sniff it, wind shift it,
people kick it, a car pass over it,
a bike run right over it.
Some people noticed but
were heading for the porto-potties
or their car and did not stop
to clean up the environment.

I watched it writhe, ignored.
Did they think it was a small bomb?
Leaving it for someone who may
notice it was gone to look for it?
Black fabric shone in the sun.
I did not get out of the car
to retrieve it or throw it away.
Not sure how I would recycle it.

I hope the clean-up crew
will find a use or place for it.
It is a shiny smudge on the ground,
an un-vacuumed ort
or restless litter
waiting to be found or re-settled.
Perhaps its intention
will determine its destiny.

Trashing Trash

Oh, I love trash
Anything dirty or dingy or dusty
Anything ragged or rotten or rusty
Yes, I love Trash.

Sesame Street song sung by Oscar the Grouch

Remember Oscar is a puppet
      with no nose and lives in a trash can,
      mobile with the help of Bruno the Trashman
who carries the compulsive hoarder
in his grimy container.

Remember we are people
      we have noses and live in a trash dump.
      Our trash piles in landfills, in toxic lumps
in our oceans, pollutes the air. We create
mountains of trash for Earth to carry.

Each year nations generate
      1.3 billion tons of waste.
      In our gluttonous haste
we will soar to 4 billion tons
by 2100–if we don't suffocate.

The more urbanized and industrialized
      countries produce more trash as a result
      of population growth, rising consumption, assault
the landscape with landfills, garbage dumps at sea.
Trash pickers scavenge for livelihood.

Many people are oblivious.
      Serial waste generators often do not see
      they are charged a hidden flat fee
for what they discard, dispose more.
Trash stresses the environment.

Waste stresses not only our environment,
        but health, safety, financial and social claims.
        Garbage causes flooding, clogs drains.
Pollution runs into rivers, seeps underground.
Uncollected trash causes illnesses.

Scavengers endure hazards
        like mercury and lead
        infectious agents lie ahead
for foragers picking
from detritus of others.

Technical and engineering solutions?
        It's not just an incinerator
        for the trash generator.
Waste needs to get collected for disposal.
We need to reduce and recycle.

Pay-as-you-throw programs,
        picking up litter in bags--
        some places commitment lags.
If people pay, they may use less
and create less trash.

People love what created the trash.
        Anything dirty or dingy or dusty
        Anything ragged or rotten or rusty
People enjoy things clean, intact, fragrant
and shiny. But when done with it- trash it.

Polluted Portlandia

Our beloved, weird utopia
has hot spots with high levels
of cadmium, chromium and arsenic,
lead, poisonous heavy metals
in the air and the ground.

Glass-making factories
are suspected culprits
flummoxing regulators,
scaring residents--
all finger-pointing.

Liberal, livable Portland is proud
of its organic life style, recycling ethics,
green environmental credentials,
dynamic art and music scene,
with car-less Tillicum Crossing.

The colored glass process
is hazardous. Glassmakers
voluntarily suspended use
of unregulated metals
until pollution-control devices installed.

Smaller glassmakers were exempt
from U.S. Environmental Protection
Agency regulation, but state
could impose its own rules,
but Oregon does not.

Portland is often called
The Greenest City in America
in a first state to phase-out coal
to generate electricity reveals.
holes in environmental regulation.

DEQ knew for at least a decade
and took no action. Tree moss
sample tests discovered hot spots.
Outraged and endangered public outcry.
DEQ officials resign. Delayed changes begin.

The EPA tells states to decide
what risks they are willing to tolerate,
what benchmarks to set,
how to reduce risks.
The buck really stops here.

Pollution is everywhere.
Think Flint. Think smoggy L.A.
No level of government
deals with the risks very effectively.
Soon nowhere to breathe or drink.

In Portland those who live in glass houses
want to throw stones. Colored-glass makers
can't blow off heavy metals any more.
Glass-glistening, green-minded city--
your walk-bike-bus-bridge arcs rainbow.

NeighborWoods

A city-sponsored effort to link city's tree-maintenance efforts with neighborhood associations.

Corvallis has a new urban forester,
an arborist who came from
trying to grow trees in Brooklyn.
He's glad we do not use road salt
like Brooklyn. It's harder for trees to get water
from the soil, but we rarely have snow.

With seasonal workers and volunteers
they'll try to make our green city greener
with pruning workshops and mulching events.
They plan a fall fungi festival. Our city tends
to lean green and care for our trees.

In Franklin Square Park they dig a hole
for a starlight dogwood. They'll plant
Japanese hornbeam, flowering magnolias,
ginkos, scarlet oak and bald cypress,
to join two giant sequoias.

Some trees don't plant well because
of the moisture at the site.
They have to replant the wrong tree
for a certain spot. Our myrtlewood
beside our healthy holly appears ailing.
We will want to replant some tree there.

Once lush pink petals brown on the lawn
whirl on the street, our spring snow.
Our flowering trees carpet our town,
soften our view and step. Azaleas
and rhododendrons splash red against our fence.

Tree-tenders trim to keep trees
from interfering with power lines
or outgrow width of planter strips.
Watering in the wet Northwest,
appears easier than in Brooklyn
or thirsty California.

Barren Omen

On
Mount
Shasta
upside-down
snow horseshoe spills luck
spindly snow rivulets drain drought--
white waves over rock seeking shallow Lake Shasta. My soul
thumps at the lake view–a pond of its former self. Hullabaloo over water sinks in.

Dry Sky-Walking at Grand Canyon West

Along sun-drenched, desert roadside
Joshua trees knob and bristle.
Gouged, desiccated dirt road
jostles our dusty car,
jars us.

At the rim, though thirsty,
we line up for an hour
under covered slanted ramps
to the skywalk entrance.
We left all our possessions—
camera and liquids in a locker.
We don slippers so we don't mar glass.

The skywalk sticks out a glistening tongue
over the canyon. The skywalk arcs--
a glass rainbow off the cliff.
With muffled feet and marbled eyes
we shuffle along peering through
transparent floor at craggy rocks below.
Both sides are about waist-high glass.
You can look for miles with tinted lenses
as sun glares and heats.

Back on rocky ground
we drink water before driving
the bone-bouncing, rutted road
to asphalt and glittering Las Vegas.
Mirages steam before us.

Some Like It Hot...Some Not

As climate gets more toasty,
people will become more roasty.

We could be crispy critters
frying fat like fritters.

We can have year-round tans.
as cancer seeks skin scans.

Landscape desiccates.
Water dehydrates.

When we want to cool
no water in the pool.

Micro-life forms thrive in thermal vents
where bigger bodies' survival prevents.

The planet will have sun-scars
with thinner atmosphere like Mars.

Escape into space remains improbable,
with fleshy forms, perhaps impossible.

Add polluted, littered air,
heat can't escape anywhere.

Billions and billions of life forms
soon will face new hotter norms.

Cheer on the tardigrade--
only creature to have it made.

On Fire

Paravoor, India

Thousands at a religious festival
honoring the goddess Bhadrakali,
a southern Indian incarnation
of the Hindu goddess Kali
gathered at the Puttingal temple complex,
celebrating with fireworks.

An unauthorized pyrotechnic display
went horribly wrong killing and injuring
hundreds of celebrants. Massive fire
from explosions sent flames and debris
raining down. Some people trapped
inside, were victims of stampede.

Most of the victims were in the building
where the fireworks were stored
and it collapsed. Smoke billowing
from the temple could be seen on TV
as fireworks continued to ignite
and blast into the sky.

Ambulances drove away with injured,
rescuers searched the wreckage
for survivors and the dead.
Slab of concrete injured some
or served as gravestone.
Burn specialists treated patients.

Many fires around the world
are the result of not following rules
to protect workers or celebrants.
I was to go to the circus in Hartford, Connecticut
the day of that fire, but I thought elephants smelled
and would not go. We had tickets for fatal seats.

Survivors and victims of fires
in buildings, forests, anywhere
wonder what saved them and why
did these irresponsibly started fires
have to happen. Why were they there
when life on fire, burns to ashes?

Wildfire Zone

Fort Murray, Alberta Canada   *The Alberta wildfires are an excellent*
example of what we're seeing more and more of: warming means snow melts
earlier, soils and vegetation dries out earlier, and the fire season starts earlier.
It's a train wreck. Jonathan Overpeck

Surrounded by wilderness
with only two roads out,
near oil sand camps
wildfires rage, thirsty for rain.

80,000 people fled.
No deaths or injuries reported
but the dry land is scorched
and oil production stalled.

Oil demand decreases worldwide.
Protesters want fossil fuels under ground.
Urge alternative energy sources
while wildfires burn. Rain delayed.

The government will pay for people's needs
for those displaced, temporarily safer.
All their equipment cannot put the fire out.
Only rain can quench the wildfire.

While wildfires burn out of control,
devastate the landscape,
people could pause to reconsider
what they could do differently.

Power Hungry

Protesters try to keep fossil fuels underground.
Power companies are urged to find clean energies.
Fracking pollutes ground water, causes earthquakes.
Coal denudes landscapes in barren upheavals.
Digging for oil and gas causes fires, leaks, sinkholes.
All foul the air, contaminate soil, increase climate change.

Wind-energy companies operate
high-speed turbines with 30-year permits
killing or injuring thousands of birds
like protected bald and golden eagles.
Pollution-free energy is to ease global warming
by reducing reliance on oil and coal.

Wind farms have clusters of turbines,
30 stories tall, spinning blades
wide as a passenger jet wing.
Wingtip speeds up to 170 mph
create vortexes, turbine-tornados.
We need to demand safety measures.

Golden eagles, our national symbol
collide with wind towers, power lines,
buildings, cars and trucks.
Thousands more are poisoned
killed by gunshots, like our human population.
We all are federally protected?

All energy producers should operate
with high environmental standards,
be forced to comply for the common good.
They want a permit for a nickel mine
in protected federal wilderness in Oregon.
Should public land be exploited for profit of few?

Power inequities appear around the world.
Wealth concentrates in powerful elites
while the masses suffer, need empowerment.
World's richest 62 people have as much wealth
as 3.6 billion people. Other animals go extinct.
Soon conditions could kill us all.

Oil Train Derails

A train carrying highly inflammable crude oil
extracted from Bakken formation
in North Dakota, traveled along the scenic
Columbia Gorge headed for Tacoma, Washington
refinery de-railed, puffed plume of black smoke.
Luckily no one reported dead.

Eleven cars from a 96 car Union Pacific train
jumped the track, zig-zagged near Mosier
near a creek that feeds the Columbia River.
Several train cars caught fire and at least
one car released oil. A stretch of Interstate
was closed for hours. Community school closed.

Tanker ships and pipelines ship oil
but pipelines do not have the capacity
to handle all the landlocked new oil,
cheaper to extract from rock formations.
Trains are pipelines on wheels, many
cars-- outmoded, prone to derailments.

The North Dakota boom means tens of thousands
of more cars, increased accidents, environmental
damage and deaths: Remember Lac-Megantic Quebec,
New Brunswick, Gogama, Ontario, Canada, Aliceville, Alabama,
Cassleton and Heimdal, North Dakota, Schuykill River, Pennsylvania,
Lynchburg, Virginia, Galena, Illinois, Watertown, Wisconsin....

This derailment fuels the protestors who said
oil should not be transported by rail especially
along the Columbia noted for commerce and recreation.
Like the wildfires near oil sands area in Canada,
perhaps another signal new policies about oil
need to be pursued--more safety checks and alternatives.

Investigators will check it out, but will they listen.
Last April they found 30 defects in track
between Cascade Locks and The Dalles
with no penalties. Result of millions of tons
of products going over this track weekly.
Toxic trains drain small towns without capacity to fight fires.

Vancouver, Washington proposes the largest
train terminal across the river from Portland.
Tesoro Corp and Savage Cos project would
increase oil train traffic greatly. Estimated .0023%
of hazardous materials that do not make it safely
to their destinations cause disaster and death.

These cars derailed about 20 feet
from the sewage plant. Residents are asked
not to use bathrooms and drains into
Mosier's city sewage lines. Traffic gridlocked
for miles, delayed and re-routed, so our natural
resources of oil can be shipped to China.

Union Pacific hauls thick, waxy, crude from Utah
and Bakken crude from North Dakota. Since 2013
a one-mile train of Bakken oil a week on Oregon side
of the gorge to a Washington refinery. Crude exudes
sky-high highballs, Bakken oil is more inflammable
than Canada's tar sands. Protections too loose.

Despite regulations and required safety upgrades,
outdated cars ride the rails. It will take years
for the public to benefit- only the corporations.
Perhaps this derailment will derail oil train expansion,
ignite more protests, so the Columbia can roll on
without oily tracks to lubricate corporate greed.

Celebrating the Planet

In our town, leading up to Earth Day
a Procession of the Species
parades, dances along the waterfront.
Humans dress up as other animals.
Music and art flare in spring sun.
People from all walks of life gather
to celebrate the Earth exuberantly.

Elsewhere on the planet El Nino
kills salmon in Chile, while in Japan
meltdown contamination caused
cesium-127 filled wild boars
to go hog wild to reproduce rapidly
causing extensive environmental damage.
Earthquakes kill in Pakistan.
Volcanic shutdown of flights in Indonesia.
Cyclone Fantals aims for the Seychelles
as a Category-4. Meanwhile,
the North Pole leans toward London,
shifting the drift formerly toward Canada,
due to Greenland's shrinking ice sheets...

Climate change and human pollution
are partners. Earth is a spitfire,
ground-breaker too difficult for us to steward?
Will people and planet dance together
or will procession of the species be a dirge.

Sparkling Water

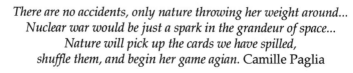

There are no accidents, only nature throwing her weight around...
Nuclear war would be just a spark in the grandeur of space...
Nature will pick up the cards we have spilled,
shuffle them, and begin her game agian. Camille Paglia

River Angels

When we flow with the river of life
do our guardian angels fly above us
through ripples and rivulets,
help us steer the course,
avoid riverteeth, escape whirlpools
to reach our destination?

Through clear or polluted,
malleable, moving water
through turbulent currents
traveling solo or with other creatures,
have they been with us from our source,
rest on our shoulders during difficult passages,
lift spirits to keep us from drowning?

Now in the autumn of my journey
do they help me swim
or ride in a boat before ice,
toward the end of the trip?

Are angels at the final landings
to wash us and hang us up
in the air to dry? Do our souls join them?
Perhaps angels whisk us into the cosmos,
orient us for our next existence
in a place with a non-water-sustaining metaphor
and refreshened guides.

What the River Carries

Sparkles of sun
        tugs of moon
riverteeth comb
        re-routing rushing water.

Pond pauses
        lagoon languishing
riverine microorganisms   fish
        bigger animals thirst on shore.

Discarded litter   oils   pesticides
        dumped from boats and air
chemical chunks from humans and machines
        which shine and rust.

The river carries on   until dams block
        canals curb   ditches direct
crafts for commerce ride   fishers probe
        bubbly bodies swim   dragging skim surface.

Rivers bridged for toxic traffic by those
        who don't want to get their feet wet.
serenely accept tourist admiration
        hope they stay ashore.

Rivers tickle toes and wears down stone
        drown   cause salmon leaps
Rivers carry whatever is thrown in   gags
        withers until desiccated to desert.

A Sheshire for Oregon Chub

1,000 to 140,000 in 80 populations

Obscure minnow, Oregon Chub
swam off Endangered Species list
and joined the newly restored club–
first fish off roster folks insist,
cause celebratory hubbub.
In low slackwater they persist.

Add to list 1993,
only eight known populations
found in Willamette Valley.
Subjected to regulation
they soon could thrive abundantly.
Many groups used conservation.

Habitat gone: flood control, farms,
urban developments, food chain lost
in eco-system that now harms.
Larger animals felt chub cost.
Diminished numbers sent alarms.
Fewer mosquitoes to accost.

Chub benefit many other critters.
Endangered others still have the jitters.

When Rain is Cold

Chilly air in our night household.
I wait for coming storm to unfold
as wind breathes over the threshold
when rain is cold. When rain is cold.

Rain pelts the leaden windowpanes.
Flailing branches fling thrashing, strain.
Power flickers, goes out again
in winter rain. In winter rain.

Inside I huddle dark, still warm
hoping to keep us all from harm
listening for the next alarm.
Time is the charm. Time is the charm.

Closing Bridges

*There is no Plan B, just as there is no Planet B. We have no intention of moving
until President Obama rescinds permit for Shell to drill in the arctic.*
Daphne Wysham

Yellow and red streamers ripple from St. John's bridge
beside thirteen dangling Greenpeace protesters
over kayaktavists and other small boats as a human blockade,
hoping to delay passage of Shell Oil Icebreaker
MSV Fennica heading for oil-drilling operations
in the Arctic before thick winter ice forces a year's drilling delay.
A gash in the ship's hull was repaired at Vigor Industrial dry dock.
As Fennica moved down the Willamette
toward the Columbia for the Pacific,
protesters increased awareness about Arctic drilling.
Supporters cheered protesters at Cathedral Park.

Thirteen protesters hung for 40 hours
100 feet from the bridges roadway
and 100 feet above the Willamette River.
The bridge was closed to traffic.
The river closed from Swan Island
to the Columbia. The first try succeeded.

Organizers were praised for creating
a visually striking scene and a nightmare
for law enforcement officers. Peacefully
Portland Police, Portland Fire and Rescue
and the Coast Guard coordinated effort
to eventually allow Fennica passage.

A US district judge in Alaska
declares Greenpeace in civil contempt
and fines of $17,500 for impeding Fennica.
Shell cut 6500 jobs and invested
$7 billion to invest in Arctic drilling
in the Chukchi Sea northwest Alaska.

Climate change shrinks the polar ice cap
making undersea oil more accessible.
Environmentalists claim the government
is irresponsible to approve more fossil fuel
development as a threat to the future.
Shell has an unreliable safety record
to extract oil from such a harsh place.

Oil spills into the sea, fracks the land
into earthquakes, pollutes ground water
and air. Oil is unsustainable.
The world is watching.

Snow Prints

on every snowfield
the definition of footprints
crumbling in the sun.   Sheenagh Pugh

On the poles polar bears,
penguins, seals adrift or blocked
by melting ice.

Mountain climbers lost
in an avalanche of shifting
sun-soaked snow.

Sleds, skis, snow sculptors
skim the surface for speed,
pack bulk before sun-melts.

Hot-headed sun slurps
the glistening snow,
drools pools, trickles.

Smudges of snow on lawns,
remnants for rain,
erasing cold.

Slippery Slope

Greenland's ice sheet is melting
at a record-breaking level
for so early in the season.

In April 2016 nearly 12 percent of ice
had a layer of meltwater
of at least a millimeter.

In 2012 the ice sheet lost
562 gigatons or billions of tons
of freshwater mass to ocean.

World-wide sea levels rose more than a millimeter
in that year alone. The vast majority
of ice sheet had some surface water.

Mountaintops nearly two miles
above sea level had snowmelt
not occurring in this century.

Now in 2016 a warm mid-altitude air mass
is getting stuck above the ice sheet.
South air brings rain not snow,

melting snow similar to 2012
when direct solar radiation caused bulk of melt,
rather warm and cloudy weather conditions.

What will happen in July and summer peaks?
Thermal erosion of cold content overlying ice sheet
means less heat needed to ripen snow to melt.

Ice sheets are slipping way into the sea.
Climate changes are heating up.
We're on a slippery slope.

Lake Abert

No outlet, 64-square-mile lake is dying. Once 16 feet deep now 2.
Volume shrunk 90%. Environmental mystery unsolved.

Salt Lake Abert in the Oregon Outback is disappearing.
Mirrored cerulean waters reflect climate changes.
Brine shrimpers, ranchers, Native Americans fearing
access to water and species soon out of their ranges.
Since the Dust Bowl the lake has not been so low.
After 70 years of enough water, scientists don't know.

Mirrored cerulean waters reflect climate changes
yet snow melts into Chewaucan River only slightly less.
Sacrosanct water rights and undisclosed users re-arranges
flow allocation into lake, leaves miles of salty nothingness.
Without food supply, migratory birds stop coming by
to the diminished home of brine shrimp and alkali fly.

Brine shrimpers, ranchers, Native Americans fearing
diminishing resources threaten their livelihood.
Cattle, hay and alfalfa require more river water, nearing
what nature puts in yearly, taking more than they should.
What's happening to the lake is not natural. They muddle.
If they don't act soon the lake's reduced to a puddle.

Access to water and species soon out of their ranges,
Scientists try to unravel mysteries to lake's decline.
Reduced river flow to lake elicits heated exchanges.
Irrigation, fish restoration need study. Environmentalists need to define
what is sustainable before off the radar lake goes dry.
Mostly forgotten lake gets saltier and smaller. Why?

Since the Dust Bowl the lake has not been so low.
Gauges to measure depth now stranded upland
100 feet from the water. Tacit approval of status quo,
fear of lost water rights to Chewaucan, loss of upper hand,
unfunded agency studies hamper solutions,
while lake desiccates with lack of resolutions.

After 70 years of enough water, scientists don't know
what they can do to help the ignored lake recover.
Lake's on road to nowhere, a place for no one to go,
a once abundant lake waits for someone to discover
why an ancient ecosystem is becoming lost
and at what future water budget's incalculable cost.

Oregon Coast

fog hides sneaker waves
skulking tsunami
perched seagull

child out-screeches
seagulls and sea lions
on dock

asphalt paves sand
buildings block sea views
solid beside waves

sea angles
wind-slanted trees
kites zig-zag with gulls.

tourists scour shore
for tsunami debris
starfish and shells

Drifts from the Sea

You might expect a shipwreck
a beached sea creature,
glass baubles, driftwood.

Recently basketballs, docks
debris from Japanese tsunami
invasive species upon our shore.

But a blue blob invasion
of Vellella vellella- like small jellyfish
which decay with a fishy smell?

Westerly winds blow, the surface floaters
containing mild neurotoxin, but don't sting
on to west coast beaches in spring.

A beautiful blue mosaic
some near skeletal shipwreck--
wish they were out at sea.

The Blob

Wedge of warm seawater called "the blob"
began spreading about a year ago
along the Pacific coast of North America
500 miles wide and 300 foot deep.
Does this signal a cyclical change?
Could it bring rains to drought-ridden California
and cause rise in global temperature?
The blob is blamed for killing seabirds
and sea lion pups, wrecking havoc
with the food chain. What does the blob portend?

Scientists suggest Pacific Decadal Oscillation or PDO
which causes the ocean to linger in warm or cool
phases which impacts sea life and climate.
PDO mirrors El Nino and La Nina–
warm and cool tropical cycles, but over longer time.
1990 started a cold phase- a slowdown,
pause in global temperatures. A flip to warm phase
can accelerate global temperatures.
Warm PDO is El Nino friendly.
Cool PDO is El Nino repellent. They think.
We still have much to learn.
Right now they think a warm PDO is gathering
similar to the blob. No idea how long it will last.

Salmon counts ebb and flow
depending on oceanic temperatures.
Cooler waters are more nourishing.
Climatologists and oceanographers
agree PDO shifts are a fact of life
but not all agree the blob is signaling change.
They question the cause and effect relationship
of PDO and presence of El Nino or La Nina.
How does the blob fit in the equation?

Meanwhile sea creatures wash up on the shore.
Salmon decline or flourish.
We dump more chemicals into the ocean,
create more garbage gyres,
dead zones and starve the sea.
The blob could derive from people.

The Blob's Companions

A warm-water mass called "the Blob"
causing havoc off the Pacific Coast.
Winter storms didn't do their cooling job
El Nino is back adding its riposte.
Die-offs of sea stars, seabirds, sardines--
other strange behaviors creating scenes.

Causing havoc off the Pacific Coast
are tropical plankton, changing native plankton's fate
Thousands fewer salmon, I miss them the most.
Sardine-starved brown pelicans refuse to mate.
Marine life engulfed in a spreading stream.
California to Canada-- losing the dream.

Winter storms didn't do their cooling job
leaving a warm-water massive brew.
What can we do with this gigantic glob?
Scientists' actions do not follow through.
Infection flourishes, food chains un-link--
changing conditions, scientists think.

El Nino is back adding its riposte
contributing to habitat changes.
How much damage can the ocean host?
Ecosystems are outside their ranges.
Tropical sunfish join warmer conditions too,
juveniles can't compete for food, starfish turn to goo.

Die-offs of sea stars, seabirds, sardines,
but Pacific whiting or hake have relatively more.
Humpback whales seeking anchovies are seen
at Columbia River mouth, nearer to shore.
Overfishing and dams add to mismanaging resources.
Stewards and ecosystem planners--join forces!

Other strange behaviors creating scenes
are tropical copepods which predators pass by
for fatter cold-water plankton. These marine
endangered natives breed late and die
So take a cruise on the ocean's ooze.
Peruse and remember if we snooze, we lose.

World With Less Oysters

Like the sand and the oyster, it's a creative irritant. In each poem, I'm trying to
reveal the truth, so it can't have a fictional beginning. Carol Ann Duffy

The world as an oyster metaphor
never meant much to me
as oysters were never appetizing
to eat and I never wore
a real set of pearls.
Life inside an oyster would
be claustrophobic and moist.

But they are a valuable part
of biodiversity, water filtration,
hosting small creatures,
the food web, habitat structure,
for species like juvenile salmon.

However, their reefs or beds are threatened.
Oysters are declining. They contain
"a cocktail of pharmaceuticals"
and chemicals–pain relievers,
antibiotics, mercury and pesticides
probably not found in ancient middens.

Groundwater runoff or waste water
flows down rivers to sea.
Harvested for human needs,
they can give us gastroenteritis
or cellulitis as well as nourish us
with zinc, iron, calcium, selenium,
vitamin A and B12. They absorb
nitrogen and phosphorus.
Quite a chemical soup!
At what levels are they toxic to us?

Over-fished and polluted,
attempts at restoration are critical
if people around the world
are to continue to consume oysters
safely or to have them available
for other purposes as well.
I'm for live and let live. I'll co-exist
with this rough, irregularly-shaped,
thick-shelled, brackish-watered, clammy kind.
I'll remain a very distant cousin.

Tucker's Tuckered Out

At Virginia Mason Center for Hyperbaric Medicine in Seattle

Tucker, a rescued olive ridley turtle
washed ashore at upscale Cannon Beach,
went to rehab at the Seattle Aquarium.

He has belly bubbles that prevent him from
swimming, diving, making him vulnerable as prey.
Aquarium staff pumped air in his lungs until he could.

Tucker became the first non-human patient
at the spendy medical center
in the hyperbaric chamber.

People use it for decompression sickness, or bends,
carbon-monoxide poisoning, for injuries, nonhealing wounds,
tissue damaged by radiation during cancer treatments.

Tucker's tubes and monitors are removed.
He will have a CT scan to see if the pockets decreased.
Not clear when he can return to the ocean.

Tucker did not have insurance.
The medical center donated its services.
Some people should be as lucky as the turtle.

Warm-blooded Fish

Scientists found the first known example
of a warm-blooded fish.
If I were a fish, warm-blooded
would be what I'd wish.

It's a large, circular fish sometimes
called a moonfish or opah.
It keeps 5 degrees warmer than environment.
If an opah, I'd call myself warm-hearted, Oprah.

Biologists inserted a thermocouple
into an opah's pectoral muscle
to record internal and external temps
following release. I'd tussle.

Other creatures of the sea: billfish, sailfish, marlin
can rise their temperature in specific parts.
Tuna and shark can warm swimming muscles.
But opah warms all, unlike counterparts.

Hundreds of feet under the ocean
where opah live is cold.
Little light penetrates that far down.
Yet opah are warm, I've been told.

Scientists found retia mirabilia
or "wonderful nets" near their gills.
Blood vessels allow counter-current
heat exchange as body warmth fills.

Veins and arteries are all intertwined.
Warm blood comes from body's core.
Contacts cold blood passing through gills
heat transfers once more.

Opah is my kind of fish. Opah keep warm.
If I'm in hot water, like shower, warm pool,
I feel heated all over and content.
Like opah, I don't need to be cool.

Bramble Cay Melomys

Researchers claim a small rat
dwelling on a Torres Strait coral reef outcropping
became the first extinct mammal species --that
melomys wiped out by climate-change, not stopping
       rapidly rising sea levels, high tides,
       surging sea water on all sides.

Dwelling on a Torres Strait coral reef outcropping
living once abundantly for many years,
Melomys faced sailors bows and arrows popping,
then human-induced environmental fears.
       Only endemic animal on Great Barrier Reef,
       now extinct is the current belief.

Became the first extinct mammal species that
was last seen in 2009, declared endangered, then
in 2014 extinct by anthrogenetic climate change. But what
about the green turtles' breeding ground, when
       will they be gone, and sea birds as well?
       Will they be engulfed by ocean's swell?

Melomys wiped out by climate change, not stopping
until 97% of habitat was gone in ten years.
Vegetation lost also, topping
the changes leaving Bramble Cay in arrears.
       Earth on edge of 6th mass extinction.
       1/6 of world species part of this distinction.

Rapidly rising sea levels, high tides
washed these mosaic-tailed, melomys off
Queensland, Australia reef. Fact hides
rats jumped ship, can swim? Some scoff.
       They are searching nearby islands
       as thorough research demands.

Now extinct is the current belief-
joins dodo, passenger pigeon, Great Auk,
Tasmanian tiger, sabre-tooth cat–grief
for Baiji white dolphin, Stella's sea cow, talk
       still of wooly mammoth, dinosaurs---
       casualties of other unnatural wars.

Acidic Seawater

Acidic seawater caused by global warming
is munching away the limestone framework
for the coral reef of the upper Florida Keys.

Ocean acidification effects
the foundations of coral reefs– a leading indicator
something is happening—earlier than expected.

The corals are crumbling, disappearing.
More than 6 million tons of limestone
from northern part of Florida Keys.

Water is nibbling nooks and crannies
making reefs porous and weaker,
dissolving flatter, and the fish will leave.

Acidity eats at the shells of shellfish,
easier prey for their predators,
harder for humans to harvest.

Ocean absorbs carbon dioxide from the air,
seawater chemistry is altered
damaging limestone faster.

Long term coral bleaching and death
causes limestone to disintegrate.
Limestone grows quicker in summer.

In winter and fall, life dies off,
carbon is released and the water
becomes more acidic naturally.

Man-made carbon dioxide
is being absorbed by the water
adding to its more rapid acidity.

Water, water everywhere- not a drop to drink,
becoming toxic to life, earth life on the brink.
So sad, I think. Hopes for survival sink.

The Coral of Kiritimati

What it really looks like is a ghost town. It's as if the buildings are standing but no one's home. Julia Baum about coral around Pacific Island of Kiritimati

Ghost towns devoid of life
on the land and in the sea.
Coral, stark, white, lifeless
haunting skeletons.

Kiritimati is part of the bleaching
due to warm waters of El Nino
and some man-made warming
on 36 percent of the world's coral reefs,
like Australian Great Barrier Reef,
American Samoa and
72 percent of US reefs.

Now algae smothers
Kiritimati's once pristine coral
with fuzzy reds and browns.
Perhaps only five percent
of the coral will survive.

Heat is killing coral.
Higher temperatures
cause damage to fishing.
Almost half a billion people
rely on coral marine life for food.
Billions of people toss
garbage into a toxic sea
endangering life further.
The acidifying sea can't breathe.

Hope lies in "little miracle corals"
one species scientists hope
will survive and repopulate
at least Kiritimati's once bright reef.

Ghost towns in the sea
can cause more ghost towns
on the land. Add polluted air
for ghost towns anywhere.

Toilet Bowl Ocean

The ocean is an unflushed toilet
filled with plastic poop.
Aquatic creatures choke,
gag and strangle in human waste
flushed to sea.

We seem to forget
we're in this existence loop.
Do we go for broke,
ignore the bitter taste,
deny responsibility?

Our descendants may regret
we did not recycle, scoop,
considered climate change a joke
and did not act with haste
to restore sustainability.

Plastic breaks and sinks.
The garbage gyre clogs drains.
Sea life ingests chinks,
disturbs the food chains
until no one drinks.

The Plastisphere

The ocean is made of drops. Mother Teresa

Plastic pieces of tossed trash create the plastisphere,
from particles of degraded plastic, size of salt.
In the oceans and water elsewhere, it's clear
the garbage patch dead zones are our fault.
We are fostering a cycle of toxicity
adding to marine ecosystems complexity.

From particles of degraded plastic, the size of salt
or glitter, microscopic creatures glom plastic particles,
leaching toxins and pathogens by default.
The subject of numerous scientific articles
creatures break down chunks of microbes of polyethylene
and dangerous chemicals of polypropylene.

In the oceans and water elsewhere, it's clear
the ecosystem our plastic detritus built
has evolved over six decades. We fear
plastic bound bacteria feeds larger predators. Our guilt
for over 245 million tons yearly of plastic trash.
Seventy pounds per person is catastrophic cache.

The garbage patch dead zones are our fault.
Zooplankton absorb additives, pigments, plasticizers, flame retardant.
Predators ingest the over 1,000 types of bacteria and algae which assault
the seaborne plastic food chain up to us. We are not vigilant
how we dispose of non-biodegradable plastic debris,
floating junk into Great Lakes and the sea.

We are fostering a cycle of toxicity.
Crabs consume gooseneck barnacles from garbage patch.
Fish, birds, turtles ingest plastic innocently,
clog intestines, suffocate, starve, catch
loss of nutrients, liver toxicity from feed.
Even seaborne cholera bacteria we don't need.

Adding to marine ecosystem complexity
bacteria attracted to plastic bits host
toxins, then bigger predators eat out of necessity
waste to dinner. Hundreds of garbage patches coast to coast,
cyclonic dead zones from currents and wind
filled with plastic particles we can't rescind.

Dead Zones

Industrial shroud cloud shifts
from east Asia, Japan
China, Korea, Russia
forms, floats, drifts
into the coastal Pacific,
flows around Hawaii
into the warm water tropics.

Phytoplankton,
foundation of the food web
which all life depends
gorge on excess nutrients,
create organic matter
sinking to deeper ocean
feasted on by microscopic bacteria,
sucking away more oxygen
that has less to start with.

Air pollution is choking fish,
changes habitats for marine organisms,
worsens overfishing,
excess dust falls on ocean coasts,
strong currents carry it into the deep.

"Hypoxic events", dead zones
with low oxygen occur near coast.
In the Pacific is it humungous
with vast amounts of deep water
a dead zone. Oxygen depletion
in era of global warming is ominous.

In Mexico City air pollution causes
toxic air and choking. Another
possible dead zone.

Ghost Fishing

They are the land mines of the sea, killing long after being forgotten. Wayne Parry

All around the world fisherman toss
or have lost fishing gear into the sea.
Garbage dumps all over the coasts
join the garbage patches in open ocean.

Traps, crab pots, nets continue to
catch what fishermen couldn't.
Abandoned gear trap and kill
fish and marine life called "ghost fishing."

Lost gear is found in sand, on the beach,
at all levels of seas and inland waters.
Technology advances rapidly.
Global fishing fleets expand.

Stormy weather frees gear, currents drag,
boats sever tie lines to keep them in place.
Solutions include degradable panels on traps,
fast-degrading screws on whelk pots.

International law prohibits intentional dumping.
The United Nations estimated 640,000 tons
of fishing nets on the ocean floor world wide.
The Ghost Fishing Foundation tackles problems.

Other projects have students picking up litter,
"Fishing for Energy" collected 3 million tons
of discarded gear nationwide. 400 crab traps
just from Barnegat Bay. Several states involved.

In Oregon we have Japanese Tsunami
cleanup from debris washing on our beaches.
Volunteers and agencies have become
ghost fisherman retrieving what broke loose.

This is not a fantasy sea world like Disney's
Finding Nemo or Sponge Bob. Not the mythical
kingdom of Poseidon. Not alien or government
undersea worlds. Divers and equipment detect this.

Like satellite space junk colliding in near
Earth orbit sending detritus to Earth,
ghost gear plummets, bottoms out.
Someday making ghosts of all of us?

Light in the Dark

Light sticks swish to music in the night.
Infra-red cameras scout in the darkness.
But some creatures glow from within
with luminescence, lightness of being
in the deepest dark seas or as mushrooms
polka-dotting light on land.

Bioluminescence in sea creatures
can be the only source of light.
They glow for defense or offense.
Light can startle, surprise attackers,
provide a smoke screen, decoy,
camouflage, alarm, warning.

But sometimes it is a come hither look
to lure a partner like moth to a flame.
Light can be a beacon, a searchlight
an aid for reproduction. Mushrooms
spread spoors to entice insects to land.
Land or sea, light helps to find mates.

Some flashes can be seen a hundred yards away.
Some light comes with touch.
Besides mushrooms, creatures like fireflies,
squid, shrimp, millipedes, pipefish, sea horses,
sea dragons, click beetles make light.
Tinkerbelle and other fairy folk could illuminate.

Male seahorse deliver the babies.
She supplies eggs. He supplies sperm.
Mix in a brood pouch on the male. Dance.
Incubate. Deliver in the morning,
by evening the male is pregnant again.
Many die due to destroyed habitat, predators' meals,
become curios and cures in Asian medicine.

Stars above reflect like light in water.
It is good to know light surrounds us
even in the darkest places.
Meditating to music and color
we seek to release the glow within us
to heal, reveal our inner light.

Spark Flight

Just as energy is the basis of life itself, and ideas the source of innovation,
so is innovation the vital spark of all human change, improvement or progress. Ted Levitt

Gegenschein

> Astronomy: a faint, elliptical patch of light in the night sky that appears
> opposite the sun, being a reflection of sunlight by meteoric material in space.

A swash of light in the night,
a reminder and reflection
of our celestial origins?

Wisdom is light. Wherever light shines
darkness and ignorance vanish. We are
splinters of light seeking understanding.

Are we trying to ignite a spark
of remembrance of who we are
and all cosmic knowledge?

We are part of creation, a light fragment
in a bio-genetic form experiencing Earth.
Light enlivens us.

Energy and consciousness--
infinite and eternal? Our light-slice
shifting form and dimension?

I will search for gegenschein
to enlighten my night, reflect
on light to draw within.

Night Lights

Flying above strings of lights
      Christmas tree cities branch.
Time to take down night lights
      and see the stars clearly.

Fading the Milky Way

*I have long thought that anyone who does not regularly or ever gaze up and see
the wonder and glory of a dark sky filled with countless stars loses a sense of
their fundamental connectedness to the universe. And as the astounding
vastness of the universe becomes obscured, there is a throwback to the vision of
the universe that essentially amounts to earth, or one's country, or state or city.
Perspective becomes myopic. But a clear sky and a little instruction allows
anyone to soar in mind and imagination to the farthest reaches of the universe in
which we are but a speck. And there is nothing more exhilarating and humbling
than that.* Brian Greene

Light pollution masks the Milky Way
for more than one-third of the world's populations.
More than 80% of North Americans today
and 60% of European nations.

Four-fifths of Earthlings live beneath
skies polluted by artificial light.
What land and sky-scapes will we bequeath?
What about future generations' birthright?

Artificial light is worst in Singapore.
Bright lights in Qatar, Israel, South Korea, Kuwait,
Canada, Argentina, United Arab Emirates-- no more
dark skies, rely on man-made light to illuminate.

In urban areas views of stars are not had
because of billboards, streetlights, signs.
You might try Madagascar, central Africa or Chad.
We need engineers with protective designs.

Some natural areas are dark like Big Bend,
Yellowstone, Dry Tortugas off Florida keys,
L.A. smears at Death Valley, but we can depend
on seeing Milky Way if we please.

The East Coast of the USA
has an obscured night sky.
People can't see the Milky Way
and light-pollution is why.

City dwellers have lost most constellations,
Saturn and medium magnitude stars,
most meteor showers in these locations.
Faint Northern Lights look like scars.

Nocturnal animal behavior is affected.
Migratory patterns change.
Altered human circadian rhythms detected,
disrupts sleep repair and recovery range.

Ancestors connected with stars in clear skies.
Their lives and structures were in alignment.
Modern folks blur cosmos, are not so wise.
Have they misconstrued their assignment?

Artificial light can focus down so does not escape
into the atmosphere and destroy sky-vison.
We must not pollute the sky-scape.
Time to make another decision.

Artificial light confuses insects,
sea turtles, birds often with deadly result.
More cosmic disconnects,
connections we have lost. Changes difficult.

Our ability to ponder cosmos, to star-gaze,
gone amid a diminished, light-polluted array.
Astronomers must look beyond the haze,
dodge space junk to explore the Milky Way.

Children will not delight in starlight,
know wonders of the night, recite:
       Star light Star Bright
       I can't see you tonight.

On the Wing

A wing is a lifting thing
a spreading, spanning action
for animals, plants, people, planes.

A wing is found on clothing
in a squadron or game position
to wing can be to wound or maim.

A wing can be a position-often opposing,
belonging to a certain place or faction,
wants freedom to fly, hope remains.

Winging-it as a wing-ding,
a party or improvising action.
Is taking under one's wing being humane?

Yellow Butterfly

A yellow butterfly with black-edged wings
flits by the window flying in blue sky.
My thoughts float to many things,
to questions I want to know why.
      Yellow wings shine like unseen sun.
      Black-edged wings like dark clouds begun.

Flits by the window flying in blue sky
so fragile, so light, so luminous,
a spot of color-- brief fly-by.
Backdrop leaves wave-- voluminous.
      Actions swish dark thoughts away,
      leaving me free to word-play.

My thoughts float to many things--
especially flights of fantasy.
I free what imagination brings.
I consider quests cosmically.
      I am not alone to wonder
      all the possibilities to ponder.

To questions I want to know why
but answers lead to more questions.
I give meditation a try
and read for more suggestions.
      The more I explore "cloud of unknowing",
      I find my ignorance and limitations showing.

Yellow wings shine like unseen sun,
but inside I can feel its glow.
I am connected to everyone
part of the All outflow.
      What insights can I learn
      as my enhancing hopes churn?

Black-edged wings like dark clouds begun
have differing densities, shapes, intent.
Like fringes until our lives are done.
We pursue our plans, remain resilient.
      Transient butterflies like us all
      who came to Earth, answered the call.

My Pet Moth

A moth follows me room to room
in my fertile fempire.
For weeks the moth shadows my moves.

It swishes across the TV screen
lands a freckle on a face
a speck on a background.

The moth does not respect my privacy-
even in the bathroom or the bedroom.
I can't see the moth when the lights are off.

In the kitchen it flies by
to spy on what I'm eating,
to see what orts I drop.

When I'm at the computer
it hovers, ready to snitch my snack
or distract me with the whir of wings.

Like a silent nano-drone
checking me out? Surveillance report
to my guides or muse?

Some moths get caught in our traps,
but a least one moth stays free
to watch and annoy me.

Is it a food or fabric moth?
A nimble nibbler,
either way I guess I share.

The moth knows I am slow,
have poor vision, and my reflexes--
well, I've not caught one.

Perhaps the moth is lonely,
waiting for friends or family.
Perhaps it is lured by light.

Maybe moths have shifts,
scouts to survey territory.
I figure I'm an easy target.

Moths have short life times.
I would not know when one died
and exchanged commands.

I'll just consider the moth a pet.
I hope it is a fruit fly and not
a clothes cruncher.

Pets can be a nuisance.
A moth usually keeps a distance.
I do not like being bugged by bugs.

A pet should have a name.
Zoth the moth- just one name
for all its manifestations.

I will miss Zoth's swirling flight,
its mysterious presence, wondering
source of its essence, when Zoth chills out.

Bugaboos

I am Linda's persistently, pesky moth.
She calls me epithets, names me Zoth.

I follow her room to room
avoiding the traps of doom.

As long as I hunt to live,
Linda's hoard has much to give.

Sometimes she's a sloth
and I rest on cloth.

Sometimes she swats at me
but I am fast and soar free.

Her eyes blur, her limbs are slow.
So really I am free to come and go.

Sometimes she laughs, calls me her pet
but she doesn't own or tame me yet.

Perhaps she thinks I'm sent for surveillance
from some supernatural angelic providence.

Sometimes she guesses I'm a muse
imprinting insights she can't refuse.

I'm tired of this vigilant situation.
I'm about to take a compost vacation.

I sent my cousin, Moe Mosquito
to buzz and bug her when I go.

Bat Invasions

Residents off **Bat**esmans Bay
in New South Wales, Australia
declared a state of emergency
when more than 100,000 bats invaded.

Also called grey-headed flying foxes,
they outfox attempts to get them to leave
despite $1.8 million to help local councils
to drive them away.

Bats are considered a vulnerable species,
only removed legally by non-lethal ways.
Methods possible are smoke, noise
and clearing vegetation. All cause problems.

Some foxy bats have three-foot wingspans.
Imagine the fluttering in the skies, bats
hanging upside down like laundry on a line
in unprecedented numbers.

Animal Rights groups urge patience
time to enable bats to move on.
Elsewhere in six years nearly seven million
bats were wiped out in U.S. and Canada.

Bats are dying of a deadly infection,
a fungus called White-nose Syndrome.
Cavers should decontaminate shoes to stop spread.
Bats eat bugs. Effective pest control.

Bats are coming out of their caves.
Not just a Halloween symbol.
They are not the only disoriented creatures.
We are all a little battier.

Nows

Forever is composed of nows.   Emily Dickinson

Apples plop polka dots on the lawn.
A mourning dove coos. Starling squawks.
Windows open to free inside air.
I type with bandaged hand.

Nows like this go on forever.
Some provoke more feeling,
as I remember nows- past
and try to imagine nows-future.

If the soul experiences these nows to learn,
and each entity plays their roles
until the curtain call for that now--
my mind muddles and boggles in nows.

As I ponder and plink the keys,
nows have come and gone.
 I can only welcome nows
and let them go into the cosmos.

The mourning dove coos, still bends the branch.
Apples fall in temporary patterns as starlings fly-by.
Windows remain open to warming air.
I remove the hand bandage and type.

Quintet for LBJs

1. Harbinger of Spring

A LBJ (little brown job)
hits morning window with crash–
dives, taps, flaps wings furiously
like Morris Code–dot and dash.
One through four knocks without pattern
repeating wing and breast bash.
Muddy smudges on our window
brown feathers flash leave brush prints.
Will not stop despite our hints.

2. Dive Bombers

LBJ
spring-loaded, breast-bumper
flies, collides, persists
illusion-chaser, enemy-chaser
lifts off, seeking, aims
lethal, delusional
bomber

3. Bird- Flashers

Brown
bird
blasts pane
bashes breast
mud-feathers window
then flies away to try again

4.

birds crashes window
pane flashes images of light
to lure breast-bashing

5. Bird-Bashing

1.

This morning brown bird attacks window pane.
Do mirrored reflections from inside lure?
Fanatically tries again and again.
Not holly for perched there, can procure.
Maybe mistakes angels in room. Not sure
can realize not another bird. Spots more light?
Images in mirror distorts–not pure.
Whatever can be seen in glass, not right
for bird's quest. Put down shade to be humane,
but paper, toy cat, still does not restrain.

2.

A poets scribbled in setting sun
another bird-tapper was distracting.
How were we to divert this strident one
from all the attention it's attracting?
Somehow window glass is still refracting.
Inside mirror's glowing light illusions.
Perhaps bird's blurred vision is reacting.
Perplexed poets discussed their conclusions.
We tried shade first. It stopped. This time we won.
It worked and we got our poetry done.

3.

Another LBJ came at breakfast time.
Is this bird-basher suicidal or sick,
fascinated by glass glitter to climb
upward from ripe holly berries so thick?
There is delight on every green stick.
Is it a messenger from another dimension
tapping some cosmic code or some music,
earnestly trying to get out attention?
I would like to think its gift was sublime,
but method of delivery–a crime.

The Knocking Bird

A knocking bird taps the same window pane
at the same time each morning, for about an hour.
Is it some mockingbird west coast relative
sending me a message before I visit the East coast,
knocking some sense into my head, knocking out fear?

This little brown bird jobber is diligent,
persists despite pulled down shade,
does not transfer its attention to adjacent window.
Placing paper, a pink stuffed cat, staring back,
the knocking bird doesn't retreat from glistening, mirror reflection.

Flicking feathers smudge mud. Breast bumping
like a sporting victory, pounds sound not meaning.
Sometimes at sunset the knocking returns--
sunrise as we read the newspaper,
sunset as we create Scrabble words.

When I see nearby nosy black birds,
I feel departed loved ones are checking up on me.
Gray and white mockingbirds may mean Northwest fog
or aging. But this knocking bird is brownish- earthy
I'll fly to the East before many spring birds return.

Somehow this knocking must mean something.
A disturbed woman knocked on our door at midnight
recently, but it was to get help for her. This is knocking bird.
appeared before a friend died and two weeks before trip.
Knocking has some ominous allusions as I face flight.

The trip is threatening when I am dealing with wings--
boarding and debarking planes. The trip is also celebratory
with family and friends wingdings. Knocking means knocking what?
The knocking bird launches from poisonous holly tree,
swoops to ground then swishes up to shining window.

How many knocks should I watch or listen to?
The beats mean some cosmic code I do not know?
It is up to me to find meaning, symbolism or dismiss.
I can only guess the knocking bird's intention.
I hope for gift of celestial light knocking my noggin.

Return of the Knocking Bird

Before sunset, brume gone,
the setting sun somehow
lured a knocking bird to the same pane
attracted by mirror, reflections.
One brownish bird, two knocks
of breast and wings against glass.

Inside poets chatted before critiquing poems.
A few poets had seen the knocking bird
on other forays with more rapping, tapping --
more sustained efforts. They tried to name
this bird I called a knocking bird--
LBJ, thrush or just some unknown brown bird.

That afternoon in a towering oak
across the street, a large black bird,
perhaps crow or raven twice swooped
an arc toward our house, then fled west.
A black bird, perhaps a visit from deceased relative
or some portent to pay attention.

Morning, a few days after our return from a trip,
my husband reported a briefer knocking bird attack,
much less duration, maybe more like
a welcome home than frantic illusion.
But my seeing a brown and black bird- each
flying twice into my view seemed an omen.

Several illnesses and recent deaths
of family and friends needed closure.
Does the fewer attempts to catch my eye
mean some resolution near.
Or the black bird shifting intention
to increase my pondering.

How does one react to unusual sightings?
How does one interpret meaning or
is it coincidence- their agenda not mine.
When I see these birds mostly in sunshine
darkling the sky, swooping into view,
my flighty curiosity seeks grounding.

Vestiges of the Knocking Birds

Before a March trip to the East Coast
one at a time, birds breast-bumped and wing-thumped
against the front window
leaving muddy imprints.

This happened daily for weeks
sometimes sunset as well as morning.
What intention, meaning, portent
were these birds trying to convey?

On our return to West Coast mud-smudges remain
on the pane, but it has been days
without the banging, spring harbingers.
Vertical etches lead eyes upward, arrow earth.

Rain, hail did not wash away
the vestiges of feathery flutters.
A balmy winter brought spring early here
while the snowbound East yearns for birds.

Just one pane attracted knocking birds.
Now flowering trees petal ground.
Somewhere amid tulips and ample blooms
knocking birds peck softer surfaces.

Sharing Cherries

We beat bothersome birds to our cherries.
They're so deep purple and sweet.
Numerous as our blueberries,
cherries are an extra-special treat.
Grandpa picks the lower limbs clean,
with many cherries still unseen.

They're so deep purple and sweet,
Grandpa nibbles many from the bowl.
In his cherry bough retreat,
he looks like a grinning troll.
He plucks and picks the branches bare,
delighted he beat the blue birds there.

Numerous as our blueberries
ripening on the ground below,
perhaps they're nipped by garden fairies?
But brazen birds–I don't know
why they have not arrived yet.
We shared last year, did they forget?

Cherries are an extra-special treat
because we are getting a bigger portion.
With pit-dropping birds we can't compete,
so bird-free is cause for celebration.
We have no noise or spray deterrent
to cause the birds any discontent.

Grandpa picks the lower limbs clean
then climbs a ladder to pick higher.
He steadies stance as he tries to glean
all the cherries he might desire.
They are chemical-free cherries so
what made lucky birds not peck and go?

With many cherries still unseen
and clueless birds still staying away,
we relish this unusually tranquil scene.
But what keeps preying birds at bay?
Perhaps they dine elsewhere unaware
we have abundant cherries we'll share.

Cherry Blight

This winter was too warm to detour blight.
The cherries are abundant but ill.
They don't look or taste right.
But the birds come still.
     Pesticide-free cherries met their match.
     These cherries are a defective batch.

The cherries are abundant but ill.
They have wormholes and quickly rot.
Finicky birds don't eat their fill.
Husband picks the best we've got.
     The ladder climbs higher up the tree.
     He chooses the cherries carefully.

They don't look or taste right.
Somehow the skin has been pricked.
One side is tan. Taste difference slight
but somehow birds and we are tricked.
     Many more cherries to select
     also means more to reject.

But the birds come still
some nibble near the top of tree.
I witness from the windowsill
as my husband picks patiently.
     Not the noisy racket of last year.
     Birds not inviting friends it would appear.

Pesticide-free cherries met their match.
So many cherries infected, rotting away.
Bruised with a light tan patch,
poked and picked without spray.
     But we will not panic.
     We resolve to remain organic.

These cherries are a defective batch
but they were very prolific.
There are enough for all this watch.
Pest-free cherries are terrific.
     Husband works hard to pick the best,
     willingly shares with birds the rest.

A Restless Repose

A bird with an unusual chirp
called for a companion
on the other side of the shade
as I tried to nap.

I am used to mourning doves
or the raspy chatter of cherry-chasing jays.
But this bird had a perky voice --
almost tonal like Chinese.

Since I did not see the creature,
I had to assume it was a bird
in the nearby holly tree. But maybe
it was a two or four-legged passerby?

Could some birder be practicing birdcalls
strolling down the street outside my window?
Some mini-drone squawking bird talk
adding more noise to the sky?

I haven't heard a deer talk,
they might be protesting the fence
barrier to the backyard, maybe
mimicking a bird to get attention.

I could have peeked under the shade
to see who the beckoning beak was.
Perhaps it was laziness I did not do so.
Perhaps I wanted to preserve the mystery.

But it sure sounded like a bird.
I could imagine what the bird looked like,
guess what it was saying. Doing so,
kept me from napping. Back to work.

The Vulture

For two days from our window we looked, could
a vulture be for the first time in our suburban backyard?
A rare inhabitant in our manicured, neighborhood?
Believing it was really there was very hard.
　　　Wild turkeys have invaded this town
　　　but carrion brought this bird down.

A vulture be for the first time in our suburban backyard?
We saw a bald, red-headed, dark, bird.
A carcass left its calling card.
Vultures prefer fresh decaying flesh, I heard.
　　　I researched vultures in the New World.
　　　This is a turkey vulture, wings furled.

A rare inhabitant in our manicured, lawn backyard--
alone from its wake, kettle, venue, volt, committee.
Was the carcass rabbit, kitten, nutria discard?
No way to know– or a raccoon maybe?
　　　The carrion became a pile of bones
　　　in the garden walled by stones.

Believing it was really there was very hard,
though I have no problem imagining winged beings.
Just a scavenging buzzard, left me jarred.
Birds, bugs, butterflies, or fairies–seeing
　　　them is somehow more pleasant.
　　　I prefer them and hummingbirds or pheasant.

Wild turkeys have invaded this town,
a real nuisance to some, but there is legislation
against shooting them randomly. They're rules shown
on ways for annoying wild turkey regulation.
　　　Would this turkey vulture be in danger?
　　　This scenario is getting stranger.

But carrion brought this bird down.
The vulture's protected under Migratory Bird Treaty.
It's unprotected red head, made me frown,
yet this bird of prey displayed a wild majesty.
　　　Then the vulture spread its large wings to fly,
　　　magnificently, swooshing darkly into blue sky.

153

Clean Pickings

The turkey vulture picked the possum clean.
At least we think it was a possum.
The skeleton looked lanky.
We thought it might be a big bird
until we saw fangs.

Then we thought it was a cat.
Too big for a rat...I hope.
Could have been a nutria.
Probably not a raccoon.
The skeleton looked stained brown.

My husband and grandson found
the remains in the garden
as they spread mulch.
We figured it was the vulture's
meticulous dining.

When I asked an animal lover
and expert if she could identify
the bony creature, she could not look.
She deals with living animals.
This situation crept her out.

So the mystery is not solved.
The skeleton is in the compost heap.
I wonder if another animal will spy it.
I hope not a good friend or family.
Should we have buried it? Unknown?

Wild Turkeys in Town

In the part of town with manicured mansions
and three-car garages, pillars and gates
on rolling acreage, a haughty, head-high rooster,
big-breasted, struts and gobbles toward our car,
near about fifteen, trim, bobbing, pecking, nonchalant,
hens--out of sight of the landowners.

In another part of town with humbler homes,
one or two car garages, wood and wire fences,
with flatter backyards, flocks of wild turkeys
are pests, picking earnestly, noisily at the lawn.
Owners request permits to shoot too tough turkeys,
not buttered-up for Thanksgiving fare.

When the officials come and shoot their quota,
they carry their carrion to the homeless shelter.

Changing Atmosphere

Contrails-- white scars
rend the blue sky,
criss-cross and fray
disperse into daylight.

Clouds conceal contrails
many days, unseen
water vapor or ice crystals
hidden, dissolve.

Grounded, I witness
sky patterns: sunrise
sunset, storms,
dynamic shroud.

Somewhere bombs,
smoke, mushroom clouds,
pollution reach skyward.
Altered atmosphere- by us.

The Planes Fly Low

Rumblings heard outside my window
under the north-south route they flow.
Not often heard as swiftly go
the planes fly low. The planes fly low.

Unseen amid dense winter fog
how many miles will aircraft log?
Polluting contrails. Airways clog.
No dialogue. No dialogue

Sounds like a military fleet
not alone, mission incomplete.
Practice what they need to repeat?
A sonic beat. A sonic beat.

Planes cast off ominous sound
and leave behind toxic compound.
Can the skyways someday rebound?
High off the ground. High off the ground.

Below I conjure why they fly
in such dense clouds, gray heavy sky.
What precautions should apply?
I wonder why. I wonder why.

Junking the Air

Space junk doesn't just orbit
near-Earth neighborhood.
Joining aircraft in cluttered
near-Earth flight patterns
are drone taxis.

When stuck on a freeway
I thought of layers of traffic
several levels above or below road
all following the routes
without congestion could increase flow.

Hovercraft seems wonderful.
No need for roads,
automated to drive safely,
dodge obstacles.
Fuel cells might add distance.

Already we cannot see the Milky Way
for light-pollution, now more space junk
at a closer range. Sky criss-crossed
with vehicles, steering from storms.
Birds beware.

Will aerial transports cause
less pollution than ground travel?
Airplane's contrails and emissions
streak skies. Space junk collisions
endanger planet. Drones attack.

When people are not driving
and computers GPS destinations,
technology decreases pollution,
what do we do with the asphalt?
Roads to nowhere?

Tele-porting could restore natural habitat,
reduce land use for vehicles
increase use for parks, food, art.
Until then the crowded skies
will be shiny, glow too much artificial light.
I'll miss the stars.

Drones

Drones buzz and whirr above--
all sizes like bugs, birds and bigger,
some endanger airplanes. Pesky aviation.

Nano-drones fly from your palm,
a metallic insectoid, mechanical bee?
No honey. Short flights, shorter falls.

Six-rotor drones use GPS for first
autonomous urban delivery in Hawthorne, Nevada
of bottled water, emergency food, first aid kit.

A Flirtey drone delivered a package
of prescription medicine at Remote Area
Medical Clinic in Wise County, Virgina.

Kind of useful if you are stuck in the middle
of nowhere, where you probably should not be
or accidentally can't care for yourself.

Many companies want to deliver goods by drones,
right to your doorstep. They'll compete with mailbox
and postal workers already stressed by digital media.

Hobbyists interfere with flights, are asked to fly low
and follow the rules. Handy way to spy on anyone.
With cameras on board they gain new surveillance.

Drone racers with video goggles, controllers
and antenna pilot drones equipped with cameras.
With GoPro you can review flight and gauge progress.

Drones zip through gate hurdles, slalom through flags.
Pilots watch live video feed to help navigate
speeds up to 100 miles per hour.

Drone racing is a world-wide phenomenon.
In Dubai a race had $1 million in prize money.
Of course, drone pilots are on Facebook.

While drones provide healing, service and fun,
in war zones launched from distant places, they kill.
They can strike from anyone, anywhere.

Instead of looking at stars we could see glittery drones.
Aviary creatures, planes, people would try to avoid being a drone target.
Drones could splat the sky, collide even with satellites some day.

Drones could takeover so much airspace
and land in so many inappropriate places until
we question drones' intentions and our safety.

Like most inventions there are good and bad
consequences. As we are prone to drone
we will need to be vigilant, look above and below.

Cosmic Dust Drifters

Cosmic dust falls to earth,
fertilizes the planet
creates ingredients
from star stuff into people,
all there is.

Tiny debris particles from shooting stars,
comet tails, asteroid collision remnants,
celestial matter in process since origin of cosmos,
form clouds high in the atmosphere.
About 60 tons a day
infiltrate the atmosphere
sprinkle life particles on the earth.

All the energy particles as well
zip unseen through us, motivate action
just gobs of invisible cosmic orts
surrounding us. We gasp in star dust
energy bits of thought, unseen particle zoo.

All the microscopic dust balls
float around, engulfed in smoke,
chemical emissions, air pollution
blurring the cosmic drifters.
Everywhere the air struggles.
When we lose the air, we are done.

How long did it take to get here?
Where did it come from?
Will it keep coming?
Can we clear the air?

Chicken Little the sky IS falling.

Earth Rings

A cosmic collision
while Earth was forming
created a temporary
red, hot, glowing ring.
Some fragments fell to Earth.
Some flung into space.
Some spun to become the moon.

Recently we created a ring of satellites--
shiny, silvery, metallic orbs,
22,000 miles in geo-synchronous orbit–
flying like bullets.

When they collide,
as two have in near-Earth orbit,
they become flying ammunition
catalysts for chaos in communication.
Too many satellites–
a traffic jam with disastrous collisions,
a noose threatening life in Earth
of our own making, the only un-natural ring
we know in our universe.
Jupiter, Saturn and other ringed planets
still have their natural rings.

Our moon spirals away one- two inches yearly
leaving us billions of years after the sun.
These rings of light circle Gaia,
shine on our metallic rings,
loosening their reins to gravity.
When will they become tired of circling
around lead like a ring in the nose?

Beam me Up?

Good-bye aluminum can spacecraft--
here come fabric pinballs to shoot into space,
with mysterious, multi-layered shields equal
or better at bouncing off space debris.

BEAM means Bigelow Expandable Activity Module
an expandable habitat destined to be launched to attach
to the International Space Station
by unmanned Space X Falcon rocket--
someday to moon, Mars and beyond.

Future projects can inflate to four- level compartments
but for now- BEAM is like a small bedroom
inflated to 13 feet long,10-1/2 feet in diameter,
where tests will be done for two years before burning up in re-entry.

BEAM will balloon on the side of the space station
like a tumor, be tested and cut-off before downfall.
Hatch remains sealed unless inspected for microbes,
check and change sensors, collect air.

Genesis I and II, expandable spacecraft
are still orbiting after a decade.
A new bedroom community of commuters
with vast yards could soon to join them.

With all the drones, rockets, planes, satellites, space stations,
natural, and possibly supernatural creations,
the space junk collisions are bound to increase.

Metal or synthetic fabrics–however shaped --
can create claustrophobic conditions
for scientists and tourists – definitely for me.

I like the feeling of weightlessness, floating -
bubbly, bouncy aspects of inflatable toys,
but hardware and software could poke and choke.

Like inside a travel trailer,
now deluxed into tiny houses,
565 cubic feet of space in BEAM
would still take my breath away
leaving me gasping, seeking grounding.

Beam someone else up.
        I'll watch the documentary.

Spark Ancient Mysteries

Curiosity is the spark behind the spark of every great idea.
The future belongs to the curious. Unknown

Mysteries

Life in this reality is not always consensual.
People have experiences they can't explain.
Not all thought is based on the sensual.
Memory records what we can retain.
>   Strange occurrences throughout history
>   add to this collective mystery.

People have experiences they can't explain.
Sightings and dreams they don't understand.
Incidents arrive from another plane
not under our own command.
>   Hidden knowledge conceals.
>   Open access reveals.

Not all thought is based on the sensual
the subconscious stirs deep in the mind.
Is our essence eternal, thought perpetual
drawing from recesses we cannot find?
>   Does consciousness come from another dimension
>   trying to guide us, get our attention?

Memory records what we can retain.
So much is lost in the brume of time.
Discoveries re-discovered again.
Our family tree branch covered with rime.
>   Languages lost, can't communicate
>   what they learned and their fate.

Strange occurrences throughout history
lead us to believe we are not alone.
Cosmic beings are part of our story.
Perhaps we are some cosmic clone.
>   We are star stuff from somewhere.
>   Of our origins, we are not aware.

Add to this collective mystery
we are not the only place where sentient life
could have generated, free
to explore or oppressed by strife.
>   Alternate viewpoints persist.
>   Rigid belief systems resist.

Before Recorded Time

How many civilizations rose and fell
erased by extinctions by Earth changes?
Remnants remain but no one can tell
stories of really ancient one's exchanges.
New technology scans land and sea.
Will we ever know what used to be?

Erased by extinctions by Earth changes
going on for many millions of years
unless time travel rearranges
no way to know what is still in arrears.
Ooparts show up in unusual places.
Accomplishments just by human races?

Remnants remain but no one can tell
who built massive stone monoliths, lost city,
mysterious artifacts. What disaster befell
these creators, quelled their creativity?
Gobekli Tepe was buried to preserve.
What function did this complex serve?

Stories of really ancient one's exchanges
with extraterrestrial powers remain mythic.
Sacred texts describes some interchanges.
Surely much older beings than Paleolithic.
Fire and ice, burn and bury evidence
despite our curiosity and persistence.

New technology scans land and sea
finds new petroglyphs, Nazca lines, cave art,
undersea complexes-- maybe Atlantis, Lemuria?
Seeking the next perplexing Oopart.
Many cultures flourished and did not last,
way before evolution theory and recording past.

Will we ever know what used to be:
their stellar origins, their earthly mission,
their wisdom, predictions, dreams, technology?
Did they discover any place Elysian?
I imagine past and future while puzzling present,
wondering at all times what was the intent?

Beautiful Mysteries

The most beautiful things we can experience is the mysterious. It is the source of all true art and science. Albert Einstein

Mysterious cosmic wonder
quest of spirit, science and art,
from the source we are all a part.
Much unknown for us to ponder
whether on Earth or out yonder.
Curious, creative we probe
with many tools around the globe
different paths to seek the stars.
We are eternal avatars
so we can don transforming robe.

Inhumane Evolution

Theories abound about DNA manipulation.
For human evolvement activation is needed
to prevent cosmic catastrophe, global annihilation.
In the past vast destruction succeeded.
> People's DNA tweaked, strands reduced.
> Enslavement began. Evil seduced.

For human evolvement is needed
to save the planet from our lack of cooperation
with all life on the planet. We've impeded
not just our progress but all of Earth's creation.
> Our theories of evolution appear flawed.
> Our rate of progression is not to applaud.

To prevent cosmic catastrophe, global annihilation
galactic energies want to pep the steps,
plug in more codes to aid our salvation.
We have free will but will we accept the preps?
> Perhaps we really have no choice to participate.
> Perhaps the instructions will come too late.

In the past vast destruction succeeded,
galactic wars destroyed Earth's original plan.
Once again we were cosmically seeded,
but we were not as well off as when we began.
> Forces of darkness darkled forces of light.
> Duality reality became our plight.

People's DNA tweaked, strands reduced.
They say we had 12. Now helix of two.
We are left with what the winners produced.
We had the powerful ones' work to do.
> Our once edenic world was overthrown,
> conquered by those who took the throne.

Enslavement began. Evil seduced.
Positive-negative struggles began.
Top few ruled the masses, introduced
injustice, inequality, violence to their plan.
> Some of this theory could be true.
> I hope not all. What about you?

Seeding Gaia

I am convinced we are not alone.
We have been cosmically seeded.
From around the galaxy groups have flown
to the Earth where they were needed.
> We are an experiment it would appear,
> testing how life will play out here.

We have been cosmically seeded
after several of Earth's extinctions.
Over time species are weeded.
As survivors, we have the distinction--
> still here, but not much longer
> unless our skills become stronger.

From around the galaxy groups have flown
to find a place to thrive.
Earth is the test site we have known
as a planet where humanoids strive
> but we are but one form of life's diversity,
> trying to triumph over adversity.

To the Earth where they were needed
came life forms or form-less beings.
Our coding sometimes not heeded,
with intentions we're not seeing.
> Many of these entities' arrival
> is essential to our survival.

We are an experiment it would appear
to see if conditions can sustain life.
Gathered from galaxies far and near,
we'll find cosmic creators are rife.
> DNA tweaks to enhance diverse races
> have come from different intelligent places.

Testing how life will play out here,
they find we war with each other and perish.
We despoil the planet from view out there,
our free will makes poor choices, won't nourish.
> How many times will they jumpstart tribes
> with their protocols and higher vibes?

Age of Aquarius

We are here. We come to put a spark of remembrance in you. Pleiadian Message

Since the Hippie times and the song about Aquarius
I have wondered about what age we will dawn into.
The cosmos is infinite and mysterious.
What ideas will we spawn into?
>> I have no problem with alternative theories.
>> I have made several in-depth inquiries.

I have wondered about the age we will dawn into.
Aquarius relates to signs zodiacal.
What concepts will we pawn into?
I'm a fan of things astrological.
>> An age of harmony, love and peace
>> where war, hate and violence cease?

The cosmos is infinite and mysterious.
This Aquarian age is also called Holocene.
People ponder these titles and are serious--
even renamed era the Anthropocene.
>> Over the years I have not seen much progress.
>> Humanity's stewardship might even regress.

What ideas will we spawn into
an acidic sea, polluted land and air?
Toxic atmosphere with minds drawn into
what is negative and unaware.
>> A time of technological advance and turmoil.
>> A time of energy explosion of coal, gas and oil.

I have no problem with alternative theories.
They say this New Age is only 800 years old,
lasts 2155 years, Civilizations have 10,000 years series.
Our 8000 years of civilization began in 1844 I'm told.
>> Aquarius ends in 2030, then begins the Cosmic Age.
>> Spiritual awareness becomes more the new rage.

I have made several in-depth inquiries.
Still not remembering past answers to renew
what is lasting of existence of spirit, the juries
on truth, knowledge, wisdom, reality to do
>> what is best for the planet this present time,
>> to unite us to what is cosmically sublime.

Stalagmite Structures

Comparable behavior is known for Upper Paleolithic modern humans- younger than 40,000 years old, so it bridges the gap between 'them" and "us".
Emmanual Discamps

Deep in dark Bruniquel Cave
in southwestern France
Neanderthals could have built
half a dozen structures
176,000 years ago.

Scientists believe modern humans
arrived in Europe 130,000 years ago.
So Neanderthals might have mastered
the underground and fire.

400 pieces of same-sized stalagmites
broken off the cave floor were arranged
into two large ring shapes and a series
of four round piles up to 15 inches.

Almost like a tiny Stonehenge--
a mini-monolithic stone site.
If weighed, the pieces would
weigh 2.4 tons. A lot of handiwork.

Red and black soot smudges
and other fire patches indicate
the structures may have contained fire
to light the cave, perform rituals, feed.

These structures are among the best
preserved constructions
of the Pleistocene epoch. We depend
on preservation to discover the past.

How many sites of distant times
have been lost to flood and fire?
How many civilizations' modern technology
has not been found or has vanished?

Chauvet Cave paintings date 36,000 years old.
These findings were 300 yards from cave entrance.
The difficult to access cavern concealed evidence
of ancient sentient beings, but do we know who?

Pentimento

Ancient art surfaces around the world
on cave walls other than in Chauvet, France.
Red, mineral-powdered hand stencils
at least 39,000 years old
and pig-like babirusas and Asian buffalo
sprawl over 100 caves and rock shelters
in Sulawesi, Indonesia.
As dating techniques improve
where will we find art and how old?

Think of all early evidence
flooded, eroded—just gone
and whole civilizations wiped away.
How many extinctions, how many beings
left without a trace, no record
of their art or lives.

Since at least the last Ice Age
humans had a hand
in expressing their views.
Now in the Anthropocene
human hands could create
the next extinction. Maybe
no one will stop by to speculate
what happened and if they do,
how will they start again?

Atxurra Cave Art

Like Altamira in Spain
or Lascaux in France
Atxurra in the Basque region
of Spain is being classified
as a sanctuary or special
Paleolithic meeting ritual place
considered in the "Champions League",
in top ten of European cave art sites.

Atxurra Cave discovered in 1929
was not re-investigated until 2014.
70 drawings found on ledges
1,000 feet underground, very
unaccessible-- will keep tourists away.
Altamira Caves are called
the Sistine Chapel of Paleolithic art.
Atxurra also ranks highly as an art site.

A buffalo drawing has almost
20 lances into it. Most hunting
drawings have four or five lances.
Horses, buffalo, goats and deer
12,500 - 14,500 years old draw awe.
Since the cave has a hidden location,
a number and variety of quality art, perhaps
it was an exceptional place for ancients also.

Rocking It

Ancient rock art statues rock it
with tattoos on moai – stone humanoids
or carved animals crawling up the T's
at Gobekli Tepe- both sites buried,
preserved artists' mysterious intentions.

All around the world for ages, rock walls,
stone henges, temples, pyramids
align with the cosmos, represent
humanity's symbolic attempts
to express their earthly experience.

Rapa Nui rope-waddle-walked
887 giant stone statues
embellished with whirls and crescents.
Some moai don red stone hats,
face inland or toward the sea.

Gobekli Tepe's T-shaped pillars
show hints of arms, carved figures
of animals over 12,000 years ago.
Gobekli Tepe's circular complex seems
deliberately buried, purpose unknown.

New technology finds evidence of civilizations
world-wide -- Cambodia, Middle East,
the Americas- rewriting our records.
Now we face a 6th extinction caused
by this Anthropocene Age—us.

Perhaps time travel or better tools
will let us look at Earth's complete list
of past inhabitants. In the future the remnants
of the Anthropocene era could be found
by cosmic travelers–aliens or hybrid humanoids.

Who will be rocking the cradle of humanity?
Who will interpret rock remains,
puzzle over plastics, twisted metals,
disgorged fossil fuel cavities, symbols?
Where will the souls of these creators be?

Ancient Footprints

Relatives of Homo Antecessor
or "pioneer man" between
800,000 to one million years ago
left footprints in estuary mud
at Happisburgh, England.

At least two children
and one male adult imprinted,
the most ancient evidence
outside of Africa and in northern Europe
of our ancestors. But in Spain fossilized
remains claim this species died out
about 800,000 years ago.

At the time there were grasslands
with bison, mammoths, hippos,
rhinos, voles, ancient horses.
Scientists dated footprints
by studying nearby fossils
of long-extinct animals.

We do not know how they lived
700,000 years ago. Britain
had a Mediterranean climate
and earlier a colder climate
like Scandinavian ancestors.
Chris Stringer thinks 800,000
to 900,000 ago Britain was
"The edge of the inhabited world."
         I doubt it.

My imagination believes in more
ancient dwellers and civilizations
caught in traumatic upheavals
and space impacts.
We could have obliterated
all evidence of ancient sentient beings,
all created by stardust.

Alien immigrants, some who could have
stayed, tweaked genetic codes
then decided to depart or remain.
We do not have junk DNA, just
un-coded remnants of past experiments.
The real evidence of early Earth-dwellers
is beyond my imagination
and current scientific detection.
Many theories, many myths,
startling stories, possible projections.

Were we cosmically seeded,
encoded stardust,
multidimensional partners,
somehow with several species tryouts?

Some pundits say Star Children
are among us to improve the planet
with enhanced human capacities.
They join Indigo and Crystal children
to create a Fifth World of peace and abundance.
A Golden Age, perhaps recapture the worlds
we have lost before we lose,
this at least Fourth World. What world
was the ancient footprints walking?

Giants

Diggers found skeletons
        of a giant race.
Puny humans
        couldn't keep pace.
Perhaps they came
        from outer space.

Even with a large skull
        perhaps they were very dull,
        found Earth hard to mull.

Maybe they became
        too big for their britches
and died young of Marfan's
        in their niches
wore out digging such
        large burial ditches.

Goliath was supposedly one
        and David supposedly won.
        Soon all the giants were done.

Perhaps the giants
        were smart.
found Earth
        falling apart.
knew it was time
        to depart.

Submerged

Supposedly submerged ancient knowledge
can be found in hidden caches
underground and inside the Earth.

Supposedly there are 120 middle and inner earth cities:
Telos in Mt. Shasta, Posid in Brazil, Shonshe in Tibet,
Rama in India and the Agartha Network.

These humanoids live with 5th-7th dimensional consciousness
since before Lemuria and Atlantis submerged.
Surface dwellers need the same level of consciousness to stay.

Supposedly humans who want to go to 5D New Earth,
can learn to raise their consciousness and frequency
to pass through the portals or stargates.

So much ancient knowledge was lost
in past extinctions. When Earth renewed,
starseeded life returned to replenish.

Supposedly our DNA records our lives
encodes our possibilities each life
we experience for Akashic records.

So much is submerged—out of sight and sense.
We are multidimensional, but focus
on this 3D duality reality with limited equipment.

Supposedly our dreams hold clues, but all
realities are illusions we create. I'd like
to uplift all we submerge into light.

Pyramid and Pipes and China

Oops! Another Oopart
an out-of-place artifact
before civilization presumed to start
frustrates scientists finding a new "fact".

When prehistoric objects
show advancement incongruous with time,
a conventional scientist rejects,
alternative theories as not prime.

In China's Qinghai Province
three caves filled with iron pipes–
150,000 years old! They try to convince
it's not possible for perceived primitive types.

Were they built by ancient humans?
Pipes range in size–some smaller than toothpicks.
Pipes went to salt-water lake. Chinese countryman's
ingenuity? The thermoluminescence time sticks.

Eight percent of pipes contain material
not found on planet Earth.
Could the source be aerial?
Maybe from an alien berth?

If not of cosmic origin,
the scientists must reevaluate.
Culture must be older to their chagrin.
The discovery sparks debate.

Then add, these caves are amid
(a place people came to 30,000 years ago),
with pipes inside a mysterious pyramid
and no human records they know.

Radioactivity is in these pipes' structure.
They cite maybe some lost technology
of people from a very ancient culture.
No technology in the area today or in mythology.

Pipes go to a salty lake–
a twin freshwater lake is nearby.
Did the ancients make a mistake?
Also stones shaped like pillars, wonder why?
Intelligent beings built these things–
seems to be the consensus so far.
Part of the past of human beings
or aliens from a distant star?

St. Lucia Cries Her Eyes Out

From this higher realm, I can reflect
upon my earthly incarnation and aftermath
when I was called St. Lucia
"Saint of light" or as Dante wrote
"One of the supernal light."
My path to sainthood was rough.

In 300 AD Sicily I was a wealthy
young woman engaged to a Nobleman.
When my mother was miraculously cured,
I became a Christian.
I went a little compulsive with charity work–
even giving away my wedding gifts.
This angered my fiance with control issues.
He accused me of being a Christian.
Then I was jailed.

Since I would not repent my faith
the Romans tortured me–
white-hot iron spears gouged my eyes.
When my eyesight restored,
I really spooked people. They feared me.
So they tried to burn me,
but I survived unscathed.
This really freaked folks.
It took a magic sword to kill me.
But since I was credited for two miracles
and because of my devotion, I became a saint.

Christian missionaries went north with my story.
I manifested on a ship from Ireland to Sweden
as a white-robed maiden encircled with light.
I gave food to starving Swedes
in the midst of a famine.

Pre-Christian Swedes were sun-worshipers.
Even today they have poor church attendance
in summer. They want to be in the sun.
Their pagan rituals meshed with Christian
so when Swedish Christianity shifted
from Catholic to Lutheran, they still
remembered me and kept my light alive.
The Vikings venerated me with my own special day.
St. Lucia Day on December 13th
the longest night of the year
to celebrate light with festivities.

Artists depict me with light-headed halo
dress angelically in white holding a lamp or torch.
Churches crowned Lucia Queens.
A head-wreath of lingonberries
with seven candles glows like a halo.
Now in the angelic realm, this halo
variation is not especially a fashion statement
for they have their own luminous source.
However, the earthbound Lucias now
have twisty light-bulbs circling their heads–
quite a bit safer than real lighted candles.

My legend is one of generosity
and bringing light. Young girls
imitate me wearing these illuminated
crowns and white gowns, tied with red sash
to symbolize the magic sword's bloody slash.
They are assisted by white-robed Star Boys
wearing hats like pointy dunce caps
holding a stick with a star on top.
They carry breakfast buns- lussekatter
and coffee on a tray to their parents.

My spirit spread from homes, hospitals,
churches, community, schools and offices
bringing light-filled good deeds.
Lucias have beauty contests
to become Lucia Queens.
They have music, merry-making,
charity events in my honor.
Star Boys are their escorts.

I suppose some of my essence remains,
focusing on light, not my gory past.
Modern Lucia replicas do not face
my original bloody obstacles to choice.
The lure of light endures. My day, a precursor
to Christmas and Festivals of Light.

As I gaze at my sprinkled light
illuminating the Earth, I see the need
to dazzle darkness. When I contemplate
another incarnation, moving on from
my stint as a saint to a more light-filled
place than Earth, with glut of artificial light
not light generated within–
I cry my eyes out over Gaia's pain,
caused by people of faith or no faith.
I am proud of my light-bearing heritage,
enlightening Earthlings--
for at least a little while.

Guardian Sparks

Instead of relying on a situation to turn around on its own, be the positive spark that a situaion needs to change from negative to positive. Anuray Prakesh Ray

185

Sonnenizio for Earth

Earthward from the cosmos, non-earth beings arrived
on Mother Earth or Gaia for earthly manifestations.
Earthbound earthfolk, earthstars, earthworms,
other earthen creations relished their earthiness,
unearthed the bounty of this beautiful Blue Earth,
warmed their hearths, sustained their earthy essence.

Earthly-minded, earthen-hearted souls inearthed.
Earthlings plundered the Earth-Goddess.
Earthmovers constructed earthworks–
earthborn creatures unearthing chaos earth-wide.
We seek Earth-like planets since our earthiest advocates
witness earthquakes and earth-shaking events on Yearth.

The dearth of earth's stewardship could lead
to no earthlight in an Earth-less universe.

Hippie Messages Still Hip Today

Ask questions. Dig deeper diversely.
Be skeptical. Don't accept surface.
Do your own research. Does it effect adversely?
Look for peaceful solutions. Present positive face.
> Be good stewards of the Earth.
> Love-ins: In everyone, find worth.

Be skeptical. Don't accept surface.
Look at situations from other points of view.
Some conditions we should erase
and not follow what others do.
> Sometimes we are the different drummer.
> Find ways to be your own strummer.

Do your own research. Does it effect adversely
other life forms, enhance your understanding
or help us think more transversely?
Are your standards high, demanding?
> Will you find your thoughts unlock
> or do you follow shallow flock?

Look for peaceful solutions. Present positive face.
Seek to avoid violence, negativity and war.
Our past record is frankly a disgrace.
Can't we do better than we have before?
> "Give peace a chance" most folks chant.
> Why fight for greed or to be dominant?

Be good stewards of the Earth.
Not polluters and exploiters.
Protect life. Sustain Gaia's hearth.
Be guardians. Be annointers.
> This planet holds our heart and soul.
> Each of us plays a crucial role.

Love-ins: In everyone find worth.
Treat all with kindness and respect.
Join in humanity's vibrational rebirth.
Remember we all connect.
> I love being a hippie
> shouting Yes! and Yippie!

187

Do We Really Know...

bees, bats and birds die
by the millions and billions.
Wildlife populations plunge.

Ice caps melt, the ocean acidifies,
polluted aquifers deplete.
Deforestation. Habitats lost.

How are we to grow food
enough for all with drought, soil depletion,
GMO, Monsanto and toxic farming practices.

Natural gas fracking, fossil fuels endanger
environment. Industrial pollution hazards
threatened body, land, water, air.

Human rights violated by war, prisons,
immigration, injustice. Exploitation,
slavery, gender and racial discrimination.

Drugs numb reality where we gasp
for breath, eat toxic foods,
succumb to preventable and caused illness.

There are so many people out of control,
too few living sustainably
too few working on solutions and alternatives.

Do we really know where this all leads?
Do we understand the consequences?
Do we really believe the end can happen?

Pole Shift

One day the North Pole tilts to a rakish angle
flirts with chaos to the tipping point
topsy-turvy, flip-flip, upside-down.

Fire and water lick the land.
Tectonic plates break.
Life drowns and incinerates.

Electronic "cloud" drifts into space
to join greater "cloud of unknowing."
No hands hold devices earthward.

Briefly some people were relieved
they were not personally responsible
for the climatic change.

A greater force took command,
replaced their role
as stewards of the planet?

Does consciousness shift to another dimension
or a luckier plane of existence?
Just where would our essences go?

Surviving the Anthropocene

For the past 12,000 years
scientists have called this epoch
the Holocene or Greek for "entirely recent".
How long will this era last?
Will Holocene become a holocaust
for people like some other extinct species?

Some scientists call the Holocene
the Anthropocene, "Age of Humans"
because of the planetary impact our species
has on climate change, global warming,
pollution of air, land and sea,
altering the Earth's sustainability.

When astronaut John Grunsfeld
looked down from orbit, there was no place
on Earth without the mark of humans.
He also uses the term Anthropocene
"because we're intelligent
enough to recognize it."

Advocates for the Anthropocene
name change for our era, first heard the term coined
by Nobel Laureate Paul Crutzen in 2000.

Geologists often use what they call
a golden spike to mark specific time periods.
Actually they insert a bronze disk
in the rock layer to point out
where one time period ends
and another begins.

Andrew Kroll states " humans have become
a geologic force on the planet. The age
we are living now is really distinct."

W. John Kress said "It's going
to be a layer of plastic that covers the planet
if not a layer of heat trapping carbon."
>Kress likes the term Anthropocene
>because it combines the scientific
>and cultural in one word.

Anthropocene is a garbled mouth-full to pronounce
but shouldn't humans be held responsible for our actions?
Are we guardians or destroyers of this 3rd rock from our sun?
Kress believes, "never in its 4.6 billion year old history
has the Earth been so effected by one species
as it has been affected by humans."

The Age of Humans created climate change,
ozone loss, disruption of nitrogen and phosphorus cycles
causing dead zones, toxic chemical emissions and dumps,
>warfare waste and radiation, water shortages and pollution,
>acidification of the ocean, endocrine disruptors, deforestation,
>inequity in opportunity and wealth, oppression.

For Anthropocene to supplant Holocene requires approval
from the International Union of Geological Sciences Commission
on Stratigraphy. A committee decides when it started?
>We are so anthropomorphic in our worldly regard
>I am surprised Holocene was not changed
>with the advent of the Industrial Revolution.

All our high-tech wars and invasions into space
with energy fuel discharges and whizzing satellites
beaming communications into the cosmos and on Earth--
>cause orbital traffic jams and collisions
>drop debris, create capacity and speed limits--
>lots of gleaming, metallic hardware discards.

Barring some cataclysmic cosmic or earth-based extinction,
what if extra-terrestrials come? Will it become the Age of Aliens"
and "cene" with their home base? Takeover a junkyard?
>Will we be alienated from Earth
>to such an extent we start an Anthropocene
>somewhere else in the multiverse?

Will we have a future escape route mapped out
and the equipment to get there? How long
will the Anthropocene last..........anywhere?

What Does the World Need?

The world needs your creativity
Your fire of ideas
Your spark of divinity

Pati Pray Mari

If we do indeed have a spark of divinity,
what would we fire our ideas about?
How would we use our creativity
to bring innovation not doubt?
      There are many different opinions
      among the world's billions.

What would we fire our ideas about?
We do not have a lot of consensus.
We face climate change, increasing drought.
How long will it take to come to our senses?
      What challenges should take priority?
      How do we also serve the minority.

How would we use our creativity?
What areas need urgent attention?
Will we confront negativity?
What to let go? What deserves retention?
      People are only part of the equation,
      fraught with conflict, need persuasion.

To bring innovation not doubt
requires commitment and exploration
trying our best to figure out
why we have this global frustration.
      Amid such diversity, can goals unite?
      Out of darkness, can we find light?

There are many different opinions
leading us down fragmenting paths.
We need some leaders, not minions
some positive aftermaths.
      The scale of the situation is immense.
      Time for all to get off the fence.

Among the world's billions
many continue to hope.
Some say the turning point is millions
who will find new ways to cope.
> Perhaps humanity will cause their end
> and not make this planet their friend.

Chips Off the Old Block

I think the most interesting parts of human experience might be the sparks that come from that sort of chipping flint of cultures rubbing against each other.
Barbara Kingsolver

When there are chips off old block,
damage to Palmyra due to war,
clashing theories, ideas that lock
we could get stuck in what had before.
>Sparks can result in something new.
>Is that something cultures could do?

Damage to Palmyra due to war,
empires and art treasures destroyed.
We could have saved them, learned more,
if peaceful methods were employed.
>Chips from ancient buildings and art.
>Chips from curiosity and heart.

Clashing theories, ideas that lock
can lead to conflicts, intolerance.
How about some thoughts that rock
and give innovation a chance.
>Chips which reveal and show.
>Chips which help us to know.

We could get stuck in what had before,
then what would be the rub--
never to advance or find common core,
lead by cooperation or the club?
>Chipping flint of cultures could create
>if we could all openly participate.

Sparks can result in something new,
something to move life forward.
Chips can be restored, review
the goals we are moving toward.
>Chips of ice. Sparks of fire.
>Chips to nick. Sparks to inspire.

Is that something cultures could do?
Responsibility of individual?
If we take all-is-connected point of view,
what is chippings' residual?
>We need to make chips' distinction.
>As chips fall can mean extinction.

Humanity's Prospects

What is the next step in human evolution?
Does it require tweaked DNA?
Can we act in time to find resolution?
Is a dimensional shift on its way?
      Can our 3D frequency vibrate higher?
      Will we be hybrids or join angel's choir?

Does it require tweaked DNA
to bring about enhanced changes?
Aliens have encoded us, some say.
Could we make sentience exchanges?
      Can body and soul align?
      Would the world be more benign?

Can we act in time to find resolution
or will end time make our time line short?
Will we experience mutation, painful pollution?
Just what strategy is our last resort?
      How much evolution is effected by outside us
      and what changes are necessary inside us?

Is a dimensional shift on its way
guiding us into a fifth dimensional world?
Will we resonate enough to join this array
as a new Earth is unfurled?
      Will everyone leave the Old World behind
      and what future would they find?

Can our 3D frequency vibrate higher
to unleash a new reality to exist?
Will we be a believer or a denier?
Will we want it or will we resist?
      The best plan can have glitches
      filled with lovers, givers, takers, snitches.

Will we be hybrids or join angel's choir?
Humans are very unpredictable folk
capable of getting caught in a quagmire.
Can all release attachment to 3D yoke?
      How much help will we get–from where
      and what could it be like when we get there?

Time of Extremes

Gregg Braden says this is a time of extremes--
big changes as we experience three cycles' convergence.
Climate, economics and conflict change themes
calling us to develop resilience,
        resist competition for cooperation,
        employ connection not separation.

Big changes as we experience three cycles' convergence
driven by natural rhythms of the universe.
Science supports indigenous wisdom. After this divergence,
we can't go back. Things will get worse.
        There are no blueprints or guidebooks to show
        the way, but we must think differently as we go.

Climate, economics and conflict change themes--
we must survive and thrive in a new normal.
Systemic changes, old approaches rip at seams.
We must be honest, truthful and self-actual.
        Can we embrace new things when we cling to past?
        Time to think globally if humanity is to last.

When one cycle ends and another begins
is the choice point - deck stacked in our favor,
these 5125 year cycles have buffers within.
Earth's epics have energy changes to savor.
        Planet wobbles, tilts, warms and cools.
        Discover the rhythms and determine rules.

Science supports indigenous wisdom, after this divergence.
Systemic shifts have been predicted.
We cannot expect a miracle, deliverance
to escape what nature has inflicted.
        Determine how to respond in healthy ways
        as this time of extremes spreads overlays.

Can't go back. Things will get worse.
We are vulnerable and susceptible to changes.
Lives and world will have to rehearse,
creatively explore our new ranges.
> We need to think and act differently.
> Most people sense this inherently.

There are no blueprints or guide books to show
how each of us plays our part.
We need our passion and gifts now.
We develop resilience from the heart.
> Brain and heart's "little brain" can marry.
> We have a heavy load to carry.

The way? We must think differently as we go.
The ancestors knew cosmic cycles existed,
they adapted and passed on their know-how.
Despite cyclic setbacks they persisted.
> Political, religious, and corporate agendas' pain
> should be transformed and not return again.

NEWS

North East West South
combined to become NEWS.
Swen too Nordic?
What' snew too hippie?
I like wens.

Watching news
with global snafus,
requires protective
harmless cysts
around my heart.

Hot or cold topics
polar or tropics
what is news
can be dry.
Wens contain oily matter.

Unhere and Unyours

Wake up to a world unhere and unyours   Alice Fulton

After the evening news
of the world's violent hot spots,
terrible traumas, climate changes–
we are relieved when tragic news
is unhere and unyours
directly, un-now.

But fearful aspects creep
unto our consciousness,
disturb our day.
We are connected
to those unhere and unyours.
Increasingly what happens unhere
impinges and limits not just
unhere and unyours
but here and yours.

Will the world wake up
before the earth is unhere
and unyours for all of us,
for we did not steward
the polluted, poisoned planet well?
Everything was here
and yours. Wake up?

Disruptions

Gaia belches gas and fire
causing creatures to expire.
Earth rips, rends, and blasts its crust.
Her patience could soon expire.

Few predictions we can trust
but some changes are a must.
Earth's prodded, probed–gouges deep.
Her treasures crumble and rust.

Toxic levels' rise is steep.
Fuel pollution came cheap.
Water, air, land exploited.
Some day she'll make a clean sweep.

People pimple land pointed
toward extinction. Disappointed
people fail to steward home.
New guardians appointed?

Life Codes

Advocates and perpetrators of Life Code
are intelligently designing
by un-natural selection
and non-random mutation
with new ways
to tweak DNA
to tinker genes
for an evolution revolution
to cope with changing
living conditions.
Billions of people
could be genetically modified
to be healthier, smarter,
more sustainable
with alterations and regulations
needed for planetary survival.
We might create hybrids
or robot life hosts.
We can make choices
to celebrate diversity,
enhance the quality of life,
take responsibility
for all species.
Will we just say no to GMO
or save the day with DNA?

Onkalo

Spent Fuel Repository near Oikiluoto Nuclear Power Plant in Finland.
Onkalo means cave or cavity.

No
senses
detect
the radiation
so
the future
Earth beings
don't know
what's there.

Dig
deep; heave
containers,
must warn and leave
signs.
But
what can
they read or see
to understand
dangers.

Promise Keepers

Words are also actions, and actions are a kind of words. Ralph Waldo Emerson

When the Congress and other agencies
in charge of the environment refused to hear or act,
Lummi carvers made a totem pole
so their voices of protest could be seen and heard.

Protectors of the Earth and people concerned
about the health, safety and future
of all life will gather to pray, sing
and support opposition to coal trains and port terminals.

House of Tears carvers created symbols on a totem pole,
to encourage wise decisions to protect the environment,
Medicine Wheel for passing on tribal knowledge,
Eagle for spiritual knowledge, Turtle for the earth.

As the totem pole trucked along the coal train route
communicates the dangers of extraction and transport
of fossil fuels over native and non-native lands,
everyone can ponder the impact on us all.

It is a moral and spiritual issue. This is sacred land
they are permanently damaging to send our resources
to Asia so they can send the pollution back to us
over the air and sea we are also endangering.

We need to keep our word and act accordingly.
Lummi master carver Jewell James says ,
"We are all promise keepers. We can and we must,
stop this madness."

Lummi councilman, Jay Julius adds,
"The ancestors expect it. The unborn demand it."
Those living now must speak and act up.
Protesting voices of the people must prevail.

Stand Tall with Totem Poles

Generations yet unborn are being affected by the contaminates in our water...We need people to take a stand. Warrior up—take a stand, speak up, get involved in these issues. We will not be silent. Linda Soriano

Native American Lummi House of Tears carvers
carved a 22-foot totem pole to oppose proposed
coal export terminal on their nation's sacred land.

Totems are symbols of strength and wisdom.
Tribes brought totems to places in crisis like 911,
disasters like tar and mining sites and oil pipe lines.

This totem is to raise awareness and opposition
to the ecological, cultural and socio-economic threat
the extraction and export of oil and coal which concerns us all.

The totem pole is traveling along the coal train route.
Communities en route will gather to learn about
the permanent damage to the land and people.

Symbols carved into the totem encourage wisdom
in decision making about the Earth, transfer of tribal knowledge
with the Medicine wheel, turtle represents the earth.

Most ironic is the flying eagle indicating spiritual knowledge
which is also our national symbol which has betrayed
these stewards trying to stand tall for us all.

The 5,100 mile route goes from Canada, through four states.
BC Kinder Morgan plans to ship 400 tankers of heavy crude oil
refined at Kitimat to Asia. Cherry Point would be biggest coal port.

Cherry Point is on Lummi land. Other terminal
at Port of Morrow on the Columbia River.
Roll on Columbia with coal dust and oil spills!

Coal will contaminate air, drop as acid rain, leak into ground water,
destroy fishing, contribute to green house gas, break treaties,
harm sacred sites, lessen health and safety.

Coal burned overseas comes back as mercury pollution
in fish, contributes to climate change, destroys Mother Earth.
We must stand tall with totems or perish.

At the end of its journey the totem will stand
on the Cheyenne Nation Reservation in Montana
which faces expanded coal exploitation.

Evolving Earthlings

What fun to imagine a new human body!
What tweaks could come to DNA?
Some say we'll evolve from carbon to silicon,
become luminous and lighter in every way.

In lighter form we'd live on prana or light.
We'd commute multi-dimensionally.
No worries about excretions, disease,
free spirits with fewer hassles intentionally.

Many creatures have qualities I admire–
keener senses, sleeker design.
Aren't dolphins smarter, four-legged ones faster?
Many forms are more mobile than mine.

I'd like a kangaroo's handy pouch–
no pocketbook, hands kept free.
When tired lean back on sturdy tail.
I'd be a bouncier, more adaptable me.

We might develop hybrid, robotic clones
to handle conditions on Earth and in space,
use less resources, resist pollution,
abolish violence, enhance human race.

I'd design some creative thought processes
in a resilient vehicle, durable not shoddy,
become healthy with an uplifting attitude.
What fun to imagine a new human body.

Reversals

Pakistan's most populous province
approved a law to give women
protection from abusive husbands.

The Council of Islamic Ideology
opposed, basing their opposition
on Koranic teaching and Sharia Law.

It is un-Islamic for women
to leave abusive husbands
to seek refuge in a shelter.

Husbands should be allowed
to "lightly beat" their wives
if she defies his demands.

She must dress as he desires, must
have intercourse without any religious excuse,
bathe after intercourse or menstrual periods.

She must cover her head and face in public,
never interact with strangers, speak loud enough
to be heard or give monetary support without his consent.

What if wives could abuse husbands
with impunity, whip them "lightly" into shape,
demand performance or get Viagra?

Men must bathe after sweaty workouts,
cleanse genitals after sex, shave or
go shirtless if she requests.

He can't refuse to pay child support,
not perform financial and domestic duties.
He must obey her every wish and command.

Men must use a condom and not leave
birth control entirely to her,
with no religious excuse.

He must behave gentlemanly and kindly
at all times- in public or at home,
his indiscretions splayed on social media.

He will be her trophy, domestic staff,
exploitable monetarily and socially
as she requires. Speak when spoken to.

If a husband leaves the family for any reason,
he will be hunted down and legally forced
to resume his responsibilities obediently.

Variously-gendered and same sex couples
are often exempt from religious rules because
they are excluded and often cannot even marry.

It would be best if all genders treated
each other non-violently with love and respect,
with equality of choice and mutual support.

No more acid throwing, stoning, genital mutilation,
lack of access to positions of power or no control of fertility.
Until all people are empowered, religion fails.

Facing Evil

ISIS is selling sex slaves
over Facebook and Twitter
using social media for evil.

A photo and price is posted.
Facebook tries to shut sites down
but other Jihadist accounts open up.

Abu Assad Almani posted: "To all bros
thinking about buying a slave,
this one is $8,000." Slavery still exists.

One account is thought to be a German
fighting for the Islamic State, as his
country tries to aid refugees.

Social media sites used by
Islamic State Fighters have rules
allowing sex with prepubescent prisoners.

Slaves can be traded by cash-strapped soldiers,
when food and medicine are short.
Slaves can be beaten into compliance.

Ancient Islamic traditions defend this practice
as long as women are non-Muslims
captured in battle or apostate Muslim sects.

Just from Kurdish Yazidi towns
1,800 women and girls were taken.
Terrorists have abducted many more.

As the war rages, women are in cross-hairs
unsafe on any side of the conflict.
Human Rights Watch can only watch.

Gathering the Anthropocene Witches

Do not get lost in grief. Ride your power, disturb the air; be the witch, the
shocking voice of truthful stories that shatter the status quo. Protest, refuse,
fight for a new equality that places Mother Earth in the center.   Rose Flint

Anthropocene witches, come out of your covens!
Release myths and superstitions
and use your wisdom to save the world.
Rage, roar and rule over land, sea, air.
Time to become the modern wise women
of the "Age of Humans" to steer us away
from a sixth extinction of our own doing.

We do not need Halloween to get into action.
Get out your broomsticks and sweep up this world.
Someone has to clean up this mess.
You might need a super-duper vacuum cleaner for this job.
Your children and familiars could be the next victims
if we do not get our house in order.

Can we act fast enough, fly forward with courage
and commitment, bristle with new ideas?
We are caught in the Great Acceleration.
So many of us (maybe we could slow the birth rate?)
using so many resources (maybe we could live
more simply, equitably with less greed?).
So quickly we are changing the planet's sustainability.

Look outside your cauldron! Brew some new ideas
to heal the disruption in biology, chemistry and geology
of the carbon and nitrogen cycles changing the way water moves.
Carbon dioxide is at the highest level in 15 million years.

Prepare for a global trip! Gather your gear!
Have your Wicca Handbook handy for incantations,
magic spells, power-raising, protection and healing.
Don't forget your witch's cross, life and health symbol,
the apple-core pentacle of Earth Mother. She needs help.

Bring your witch's charm, your magic knot.
Might come in handy. Remember when they believed
witches control the winds, raise storms, influence weather
by making knots with our hair? Humans create their own storms.
We can't cause falling water by combing our hair.
If we could we'd need a formula for a magical conditioner and purifier.
Might bring a runic swastika for magical regeneration.
Perhaps your witches foot to stamp, to reverse man's true nature.

Broom Amazons, bring your broomsticks!
Perhaps we can sweep the threshold to repel evil,
jump the broomstick for a clean sweep.
Ride over crops to increase fertility.

Shall we mount our magical steeds, show we are not afraid
of running water, move the broom across water for good luck.
With the acidification of the oceans, depletion of ground water,
creation of dead spots where only algal blooms grow,
the wastrels need our luck and magic.

How about a black lamb for necromancy
to predict future climate changes? Find solutions?
Witches have been scapegoats for crop failures,
madness or unacceptable ideas.
Jung saw witches as projection of the dark side
of animals or female side of human nature.
Women are the light side. His thoughts are unenlightened
as belief witches swallow children
based on the fear of being devoured by mothers.

We will need space suits to breathe and avoid toxins,
probably board a spacecraft at times.
Near-orbit traffic jams and collisions a possibility.
We must be alert for the ditching satellite
and contrails scratching the sky.
They accuse us of closing up throats,
mouths, eyes and other body parts by knots
and immobilize sexual function. Might be useful in birth control
and to sieve pollution...if we could we'd help all breathe.

We do not summon demons, people do.
We are free agents, not servants of the devil.
Let us use the crack between worlds to let the spirits through.
Crack open change and sustainable commitment.
Before people create their May Day, perhaps
we can weave some spells, invocations, magical circles.
Can we intersect some interlacement patterns
a pattern line- endless and gateless barrier against evil
influences, magical protection for anything inside,
knitting all together in symbolic communion?
A new world wide web. We are the good witches.

Remember the witch hunts which slaughtered
millions of women for five centuries. The bloodshed
foundation of modern patriarchal society whose
waste, destruction and excess may end us all?

Speak out witches for nurturing! Remember when
a woman fondling a pet was suspected of witchcraft.
She was burned for keeping cats, caring for lambs,
talking to frogs, raising colts, having mice in the house
or toads in the garden. Gaia needs nurturing.

Bring your bats and cats–any pet welcome on this ride.
Humans never succeeded in telling familiars from ordinary animals.
The owl embodies wisdom and mortality. Humanity needs a dose.
Witch is a word that attracts and repels, frightens and fascinates.
The name for wise woman or witch and owl
are the same in Latin or Italian. We hope witches can rescue us.

Witches invoked the goddess by "drawing the moon",
checking moon phases for plantings,
weddings and animal management.
Come out of retirement! Biodiversity declining, wildlife halved,
agriculture irrigates and homogenizes.

Women in black, pitch the pointed hat!
Go shopping for more colorful, practical garb!
Witches are associated with black, the underworld
like mined coal gouging holes in the earth,
undermining stability, fueling dirty air.
Witch-finders accused witches of suckling demons,
stripped women to find devil's marks.
Men pricked women with sharp instruments
like penetration of earth for oil.
If deforestation continues we might lose our broomstick source
and have to ride plastic broomsticks, drones or hovercraft
which are not green machines. Prepare to upgrade your brooms!

Remember we are not hag cartoons,
ugly old witches, but hag as holy women or wise women
who know the ways of nature, healing, divination and civilized arts.
Modern witches are the 21st century's healers,
hope for those who do not know where to turn.
Wicca empower and provide sacred magic.

We can be Anjana witches who take the form
of old women to test the charity of human beings
when really they are beautiful young blue-eyed blondes,
wearing tunics of flowers and silver stars, green stockings
carrying a golden staff. They watch for animals
and live in underground palaces, full of jewels.
The staff turns everything into riches.
We may need to live underground when we kill the air and surface.

Bye-bye Baba Yaga, the spiteful sorceress.
Bewitching Anjana witches are bearers of light not darkness.
Theh soul is renewed by fusion with "nana personality."
The staff links apparently unrelated things.
Green stockings connect to primitive forces of virgin nature.
The treasures are the spiritual powers of the unconscious.

We need Anjana power in the Anthropocene
to provide a safe, sustainable world.
Are we ready to launch our flight?
Avoid the bright city lights, so you can see the stars.

Have you packed your tool kit?
We need a sanitizing vacuum cleaner-
industrial strength- air-conditioner; water renewal tools
to deal with flooding, drought, disease, smoke, smog,
plastic particulates, plutonium, radioactive isotopes,
polyaromatic hydrocarbons, lead from fossil fuel burning,
radio nuclides from atomic bombs.

Have your bell, book and candle?
Think of the Earth as a jack-o-lantern
needing light from within us all
so all of us on the surface glow
with purifying light, lightening the atmosphere.

Witches cast your spells! Pick up your broom!
A broom joins phallic stick to feminine brush
as a symbol of unity and fertility. We can all
pick up a broom for a symbolic cleaning
to sweep away evil influences
to aspurge and purify with water.

> *Burst bubble, toil with trouble,*
> *clean up rubble, lift off like Hubble.*
> *May Anthropocene witches prepare*
> *to alight everywhere.*
> *May more Earth Angels care,*
> *join them, alert and aware.*

Cosmic Sparks

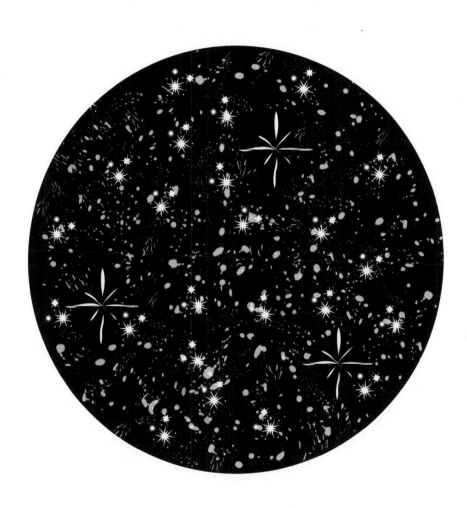

Cosmic Light-Sparks

I was birthed restless and elsewhere.   Patricia Smith

When I started splintering soul-sparks
alighting all over the multiverse,
anywhere I placed my essence
must have been with an intense sense
of restless awe and creative urgency.

Perhaps I ask, how long will I be
in this realm, in this form?
What am I supposed to learn
and share, eternally in and out of lives,
relationships, energy spilling endlessly.

As a multidimensional being
in a multiverse beyond comprehension
any consciousness trips can be
captivating and overwhelming.
Earth challenges surely are.

I cannot recall all these other facets
of my soul, for I need to focus
on my current Earth journey
to reflect light-sparks to give
this - me some glimmer and shine.

Curiosity about this reality
which could be holographic,
could be an illusion,
keeps my mind moodling, muddling,
and meandering most of the time.

Perhaps from my existences elsewhere
I could have come to Earth
to evolve with Earth School curriculum,
to get a glimpse where I need to go
for some galactic graduate school.

At some point my restless spirit
would like a re-birth somewhere
in a place of light and harmony
with creative free will to ponder anything
wherever I manifest energy.

Creating a Cosmic Plan

The creation never gives commands or demands worship because it is an egoless, nonjudgmental spiritual force. Eternal knowledge guides the growth of the universe, no need for commands or religion. Pleiadean thought.

There are several alternative theories
about the creation of the cosmos,
ancient Earth civilizations
and alien intervention by benign
beings and warfare between
warriors for control of the planet.

As a result, starseed pawns
endured tweaked DNA
from 12 strands to two
so the victors could control
the humanoid residents.
So is this part of the cosmic plan?

Positive and negative energies
eternally at war? Is the Prime Creator
a planner or anarchist— feeding
on the creations of its creations?
With my diminished capacities,
how am I to figure out what's going on?

Much information veiled in space/time mist,
is not available in this now to discover
at this stage of development.
Why would I worship an unknown source
or an entity beyond knowing?
Eternal knowledge in charge?

If the only constant is change,
the universe expanding with multiverse
with unseen dimensions impacting us,
what is a human to do? Manifested
to be manipulated? Free will just illusion?
If we are part of a cosmic plan, what's our part?

Some say Earth is a living library,
a gathering place for galactic thought,
our coded bio-genetic body holds knowledge
to plug in. With rearranged DNA
and reduced frequency, I'd like abilities restored.
My personal hologram seeks freedom.

Petition to the Cosmic Compassion Council

If such a commission is not part of the Cosmic Plan,
perhaps it should be. In behalf of the Earth Cosmic Experiment
some relief from the dark, dense, old, hierarchical energies
is too long in coming. How many extinctions
and reliance on hope are Earthlings expected to endure?

The Dalai Lama and other New Age pundits
say we are experiencing the defiant embers of a dying Old World.
Progress in enlightened, new ways of thinking does seem slow
but the light forces predict a brighter future. Wishful thinking?
Meanwhile, millions suffer and perish needlessly?

Now rainbows light bridges, buildings and monuments
to console and show solidarity with Orlando-
before it was Sandy Hook, San Bernadino, Brussels, London,
Paris, all over the world. Deranged, demonic haters
with killing machines, war against those who believe differently.

It is enough we have to deal with natural disasters,
requiring oozing our compassion, and cash, but
this misguided experiment allows people to turn free speech
into deadly action, to turn free will into domination and fear,
to turn weapons, assault rifles and guns on civilians.

Hot spots all over the world not just Middle East,
mass migrations, mass destruction, mass deaths.
Despite some hopeful movements, suffering continues.
Does a Prime Creator send life-sparks to experience
life in the multiverse to learn, create, entertain -- a voyeur?

If we are alone in the cosmos, all the more horror
that we could extinguish sentience and there are
no other experiments doing better–anywhere. Whether
illusion, ruled by a divine despot or incompetent committee–
this pissed off Earthling petitions for positive cosmic change.

Building a Merkaba

Merkaba- body of light. Divine light vehicle used by ascended masters to connect with and reach those in tune with higher realms. Mer=light. Ka=spirit. Ba=body. Surrounded by counter-rotating fields of light (wheels within wheels) spirals of energy as in DNA which transport spirit/body from one dimension to another.

What
can
cosmic
merkaba
help one to achieve?
Befuddles and muddles wee me.

By
light
travel
dimensions
across the cosmos
experience another life?

But
they're
hard
to construct
and I'm not handy.
Someone else will have to build it.

The promise of living more lightly
is a very enticing lure.
To help the cosmos shine more brightly
makes it worth dreaming about, for sure.

Cosmic Contemplation

Theories and prophecies are under scrutiny
Now all is energy. All has consciousness.
Science and spirituality are staging a mutiny,
joining to confront this contentiousness.
       Both approaches have similar cosmic goals.
       Both contenders try to define their roles.

Now all is energy. All has consciousness.
Many manifestations- lots of electricity.
How do we understand this chaotic mess?
How do we find ways of conductivity?
       Proofs are failing. New ideas prevail.
       Humanity is peeking beyond the veil.

Science and spirituality are staging a mutiny
against the old interpretations of origins and life.
Puzzlement at what's massive and tiny.
They seek a common multiversal midwife.
       How do Earthlings join the cosmic community?
       How can we find some galactic immunity?

Joining to confront this contentiousness,
astrophysicists and metaphysicists seek common ground
to solve problems and to bring happiness
with the new discoveries they have found.
       People will have to adapt and change
       their views and expand their range.

Both approaches have similar goals
filled with awe, curiosity, wonder
and try to reduce distance from contending poles.
We all have much more to ponder.
       Mayans prophesied when we're complete, aware
       we can live in the universe anywhere.

Both contenders try to define their roles
with different kinds of insight and proof.
If we are all one, connect protocols
so we won't have anything to spoof.
       Perhaps we can multidimensionally align,
       employ sacred geometry, cosmic design.

Heliolatry

Worship of the sun. Dictionary.com

When I was meditating in the backyard at dawn
greeting the sun to heal my soul and body
while causing skin cancer on my nose,
I was part of ancient rituals
acknowledging its life-giving rays,
promoting sun-worship.

Tanning sun-bathers, solstice practitioners
Central Sun Big-Bangers worship the sun.
Our local sun in its right intensity
does not outburst to shut down
the energy grid and our artificial
sources of light and energy.

Scientists expect millions more years
of service to the Milky Way
before dousing us into darkness.
But by then we might have destroyed
the Earth, gone extinct or moved on
in some form to another sun source.

While we spin on this rocky outpost
in infinite space orbiting our radiant sun,
we can give gratitude to the Source
perceived by some as an exploding sun
whose energy rays enliven each of us
to experience the cosmos.

Confronting Realities

What is reality but a consensus guess?
How many dimensions, location, cosmic realms?
Inward, outward, seen and unseen–and yes
who created all this and how many helms?
So many scientific theories abound.
Add religion to confusing compound.

How many dimensions, locations, cosmic realms?
Where does a non-tech savvy seeker start?
The factors to include tend to overwhelm.
Start with the brain or with the heart.
I find I start with imagination
and in part from dream creation.

Inward, outward, seen and unseen–and yes
our mind and body's equipment appear lacking.
Our senses are limited, technology in stress.
We need much more solid, additional backing.
We do not understand the reality before us
and do not have a unified chorus.

Who created all this and how many helms?
It's popular to appoint a singular, God creator
but I need more evidence that whelms.
There must be a beyond comprehension innovator.
Some say reality is but an illusion.
Perhaps that will be my conclusion.

So many scientific theories abound.
Just heard about Twistor Holography.
Perhaps the math and ideas are sound
but it's not found in my mind's geography.
Quantum physics, all kinds of energies–
perhaps we will discover the synergies.

Add religion to confusing compound.
But reality could be beyond spiritual and science.
Religion is constricting, I have found
with thoughts I am not in compliance.
I confront baffling realities every day
with hope for love, light, peace and play.

Beyond Human

Nootropics and nanobots could increase life span,
keep us very healthy. Drop a pill,
ingest microscopic cells, nanobots nibble all they can.
Part of us will be human still.
        As we become a transhuman, part robot
        will the soul transfer or not?

Keep us healthy, drop a pill
science is creating miracles.
We will evolve humans until
we are free of earthly cycles.
        Sturdy cyborgs, robotic beings
        can go into space we're foreseeing.

Ingest microscopic cells, nanobots nibble all they can.
Rushing through our blood stream,
they gobble disease, a complete body scan.
A fully functional body is everyone's dream.
        They are also working on a high-tech brain.
        With increased capacity, we will all gain.

Part of us will be human still.
They hope to computerize all knowledge,
input it into everyone brains, fill
souls and creativity into the collage?
        We will be full of bionic parts.
        Where will people be when this starts?

As we become a transhuman, part robot
we become more adaptable for space.
Fleshy forms tend to rot and clot.
We are a fragile human race.
        If robots go ahead to transplant and terraform
        then extraterrestrial life can become the norm.

Will the soul transfer or not?
How much remains of us in these plans?
How well will we be a polyglot,
with these cosmic clans?
        They are creating more durable, sensitive skin.
        At what point does human end and transhuman begin?

223

Creative Leaps Outside the Box

> *If you're not confused about quantum physics, that's because you haven't understood it.* Jacob Sherson

Quirky, quantum quark quests:
puzzling perplexed physics problems
leave Linda lurching, lingering, lost.

Confounded, confused, computers.
Ignore, intuitive inklings
can't compute, comprehend cosmic conundrum.

Go gamers' gobbledygook gobsmacked.
Competently, computers control chess challenges
faster, find fixes frabjously.

But befuddled blood-bodied beings,
humble, heart-filled humans
ignite individual intuition. Intelligence

(acknowledged artificial) access--
interestingly indicates in intuition, imagination
human's have headway--

defeat digital dilemmas,
pesky physics problems.   Perhaps.
People power possibly problematical.

Complex computer components cleverly
could catch up, connect, clutch content,
conquer consciousness, curiosity, creativity?

Earth Shifts

Supposedly the Earth wobbles
in a holographic universe.
The people hobble and bobble
making things better or worse
        Our universe is expanding
        way beyond our understanding.

In a holographic universe
consciousness is the substance--
part of a multiverse
part of the cosmic dance.
        Some come to the conclusion,
        life is an illusion.

The people hobble and bobble
in a reality built on thoughts.
Conflicting ideas cobble
many shoulds and oughts.
        Soul-splinters create for ALL,
        each await a cosmic call.

Making things better or worse
is a choice everyone must take.
The earthly path is diverse.
One can become awake
        perform the roles of the soul
        find what we can control.

Our universe is expanding
the only constant is change.
Earthly life is demanding,
hopes for positive interchange.
        We must give eco-balance a chance
        for all life forms to advance.

Way beyond our understanding
are origins –so much to know!
What forces are commanding
the waves within the flow?
        Can we survive the oncoming shift?
        Will our souls get an uplift?

Testing. Testing.

Earth life is a cosmic experiment.
After brane bubble burst or big bang
cosmic testing of despair or merriment,
tolerance for ecstasy and harangue,
    energized from Creations' seeds
  ⁎ to see what survives and breeds.

After brane bubble burst or big bang,
Prime Creator wanted something new
to inspire curiosity, so life sprang
with many varieties to breakthrough.
    Prime Creator didn't want to be alone
    amidst the elements, gas and stone.

Cosmic testing of despair or merriment,
yin and yang in a dualistic reality?
Not sure why essence required impairment,
but Earth life has this plurality.
    Other dimensions may have divergent tests.
    Soul-splinters could explore other contests.

Tolerance for ecstasy and harangue--
endure the extremes- like love and fear?
We experience joy and suffering's pang.
We struggle knowing this end is near.
    Do we understand challenges and rules?
    Are we a failed group of earthly fools?

Energized from Creation's seeds
with eternal lifetimes in many places
who judges who succeeds?
Can we explore other interfaces?
    What are the theories and tasks
    to perform? Who asks?

To see what survives and breeds
under these conditions of constant change
requires some stewardship, guiding creeds.
In this experiment what is our optimal range?
    Earth life's puzzle maze clings to hope
    the experiment will help us cope.

Einstein's Longshot

This is truly, I think a scientific moonshot. I really believe that. And we did it.
We landed on the moon. David Reitze

Scientists' discovery will open a new window
onto the universe. They heard a tiny "chirp" sound
when they detected ripples in gravity, some how
heard in gravitational waves. Einstein found
        the fabric of space has ripples, but undetected.
        Now scientists discovered what he suspected.

Onto the universe, they heard a tiny "chirp" sound
humanity's ears opened to cosmic music- yes!
Gravitational waves in audible form astounds.
Einstein's prediction was not just a guess.
        We can hear cosmic soundtrack and listen
        to re-shapings by violent collision.

When they detected ripple in gravity, some how
we had eyes on the sky, but no musical accompaniment.
Astronomers and physicists are shouting WOW
from the results of this all-star, international experiment.
        "The skies will never be the same!"
        the jubilant astrophysicists exclaim.

Heard in gravitational waves, Einstein found
but now proven by two black holes' collision
1.3 billion light years from Earth. Data compounds
and findings allow a new scientific revision
        like the "God Particle." Some say this bigger.
        Like the moonshot- this is a new trigger.

The fabric of space has ripples, but undetected.
A new view of the looking at the universe reveals
way to revolutionize astronomy, dreams resurrected.
Light from all wavelengths let us see yet conceals
        sound. Twin LIGO detectors' five-year upgrade
        provided equipment so discovery was made.

Now scientists discovered what he suspected.
It took a century, but Einstein was right.
A signal for massive violent events now detected.
Ripples in space-time, we can hear our plight.
        Like going from silent film to talkies.
        We now have cosmic walkie-talkies.

From the Sound of It

From the quantum perspective, all matter in the universe (multiverse, rather) is essentially a collection of sound-frequency-vibration. So to make effective change in the universe, we must meet it at its base structure. Resonant intentional hypnotic harmonics, utilizing the internal instrument of our voices to induce awakening. This is how we rock it. Excerpt from Miss Ascentia

Must be a noisy multiverse
beyond our earshot,
carrying on a cosmic karaoke.
Maybe some day we will explore
the music of the spheres-
but our planet is a loud place
from many difference sources.
Even Earth has its own sound.

If all is energy and has consciousness
we could generate quite a racket.
All the tones, volumes, expressions
of feelings, releases from natural processes,
mechanical moans and drones,
sonic booms, music, speech...
We have a lot of Third Rock vibes going on.

If we could resonate with peaceful vibrations
people could awaken, not from blasts
but by internalizing meditative sounds,
join in humming, singing, voicing om.

The Sounds of Earth golden record
voyages through space,
expected to last a billion years.
But when someone hears us,
will we still be here?
Lots of talk about how life on Earth
and the universe will end.
I don't like the sound of it.

What Cosmic Language do you Use?

Perhaps there is a Universal Cosmic Language-
Maybe with tones or with singing.
Words could flash images like lightning.

We are not alone in the cosmos.
At some point we will connect with cosmic beings.
Will we be telepathic then?

Does thought translate instantaneously
through the vastness of space
to the farthest reaches with sentient entities?

We are multidimensional beings.
When we leave our bodies for another dimension,
how do we communicate with the energies there?

Does our internal GPS go cosmic
to get to our location and back home?
What language is used in a distant place?

Is there a multiversal language
or a local language for distinct cultures?
We do not even have a global language.

I like the idea of being multi-lingual.
With 14 simultaneous lives, I could be translating
dreams and dramas in many places.

Would I communicate with a sound system,
a voice or voicelessly with some vibration,
in a symbolic or sign language?

Whatever method of delivery, I hope
I have the skills to converse, express and create
in a language appropriate to connect.

NOW?

What if ALL space-time is NOW?
Linear concepts are an illusion.
We had to get HERE somehow
to come to this conclusion.
      Light illuminates the NOW spark.
      NOW leaves me totally in the dark.

Linear concepts are an illusion?
Sacred geometry a hidden puzzle?
This reality a delusion?
I've not much to say to muzzle.
      Only abstract existence it appears?
      Concrete matters seem in arrears?

We had to get Here somehow–
some bang, blast, gravitational wave.
I shake my head– Holy cow!
Existence is an instantaneous rave?
      My body has limitations to sense
      what could be real or nonsense.

To come to this conclusion
we are but a blink or brink of NOW
only adds to my confusion
as pundits ponderously pow-wow.
      How can ALL be all at once?
      One of Prime Creator's stunts?

NOW leaves me totally in the dark.
I can't envision or understand.
Does NOW ever embark
to create another strand?
      All this is beyond belief.
      Luckily NOW is brief.

The Cosmic Game

Earthlings are not the only gang
to bang in this universe.
Come on. Just us in the cosmos?
Whether a super-symmetry, string theory,
multiverse or some other guess fan–
we could not be the only cosmic players.

All our technology, multidimensional brain
equipment focused on the Big Questions.
It is fun to speculate what's out there
and what's here–all the unseen micros and macros.
No wonder some pundits think we need
many lifetimes in many dimensions
to discover the rules of the cosmic game.

Light and energy play hide and seek.
Particles manifest, glom and smash apart.
Gravitational waves undulate and hum.
Cosmic commotion is out of sight
and not yet registered in our minds.
Somehow consciousness and soul concepts
make sentient beings semi-aware of cosmic crapshoot.

I'm intrigued with all the experiments
and theories some believe
are simultaneously occurring–all Now.
If so, past, present and future everywhere
are all Now. Are we already
winners and losers in the games we play?

Can I choose the teams I want to play with
and try to ignore the scores of other players' games?
But if we are all connected
in an omnipresent Now,
I'm trapped. My game piece checkmated,
left to cheer or boo
on the sidelines or in the fray
wondering if there will be other games to play?

Emotional Earthlings in a Cosmic Experiment

We are projected illusion in a biogenetic experiment created in space and time to study emotions. Brian Greene

We are 2D living in a 3D holographic projection. Rich Henson

Whether we are a dream, illusion,
simulation, computer program
with past, present and future
an illusion in a bubble of space-time
where universes appear
and disappear....or not--
I do not like feeling manipulated
and experimented upon,
feelings provoked and probed,
given limited equipment
and little information
what this cosmic experiment is for.

Positive and negative energy
compete for some reason
and the negative emotions
are not very pleasant
nor appear helpful to harmony
if Earthlings are to benefit
by all this research.
A dualistic planet which
plays dark and light games,
is cruel and abusive.
If time is an illusion,
has the research been completed
and we are just being studied
to see the evolvement of conclusions?

I resent an experiment
on a planet which is being
plundered, made toxic
putting the survival of all on it
in jeopardy without knowing
why this negatively is necessary.
I will try to remain positive
for it is more comfortable
and more constructive.
I will choose love and light.
I can only hope there are less
negative dimensions somewhere
whose experiments are done
so the inhabitants can live in peace.

Dimensional Yo-yo

There are 144 dimensions to Source says Druvalo.
We can elevate bottom to top and back in an instant.
I can go up and down like a dimensional yo-yo.
At what level would I be most content?
> There's a new discovery called Cosmic Grace
> that just might save the human race.

We can elevate bottom to top and back in an instant.
Currently we inhabit a near-bottom rung.
At 145th a new octave to existence-- inhabitant
of a space unknown and unsung.
> We can stream electricity to be large or small.
> Travel the cosmos to connect as part of All.

I can go up and down like a dimensional yo-yo
if I can just learn the technique to do it.
Would I then go multi-dimensionally tally-ho?
Or acknowledge that I blew it?
> Other ascension methods could exist.
> Dying's one currently I resist.

At what level would I be most content
when contaminated Earth is left to recover?
At what dimensional level can I best invent
and find what I need to discover?
> Birkeland currents and mer-ka-ba science
> are partial knowledge for self-reliance.

There is a new discovery called Cosmic Grace
which centers on a tiny spot in the heart
which expands electricity, links with space.
Male and female energies take part.
> Seven regions of the heart spark electricity.
> Ah, to live and love in synchronicity.

That just might save the human race
to experience the cosmos as soul-splinter of All
but wherever our size, form or space
we could face a challenging protocol.
> Perhaps we could become more aware,
> so we can live in love anywhere.

Cosmic Tantra

Sun and Earth have sexual energy, make love?
Somehow this theory sounds a tad kinky.
Perhaps universal sexual exchanges from above
could raise human sex above the rinky-dinky.
    Could rise sex to the sacred?
    Love could reduce hatred?

Somehow this theory sounds a tad kinky.
Involves dominance issues? Imbalance?
Model for human's perhaps unthinky.
Pathway for some intolerance?
    But this connects cosmic currents, we
    can use these also theoretically.

Perhaps universal sexual energy from above
links consciousness differently.
Humans connect bio-magnetic fields of
one, two and create three.
    When we utilize these currents
    a third is created from parents.

Could raise human sex above the rinky-dinky
if people considered sex reverently,
more love-light, immortal, less blinky
when we engage sacred geometry.
    In South America and Tibet
    some get what we don't get.

Could rise sex to the sacred?
Make us cosmically responsible?
Employ electricity safely, not scared?
Discover happiness we thought impossible?
    As we learn how to live spontaneously,
    we'll find we connect instantaneously.

Love could reduce hatred
I'm sure if we really tried.
If we find better ways to be bred
then we'd be more satisfied?
    The multiverse is unfathomably complex
    when we consider cosmic sex.

Message to the Exoplanets

Celebrate your freedom exoplanets!
If you haven't already been invaded by aliens,
watch out for humanity's impact.
A predatory, greedy species is ready
       to exploit your resources,
       dominate any living forms,
       explore your distant mystery,
       lure themselves from voyeur
       to engagement.

So while the cosmos conceals and protects
you from Earthling technology
       rejoice in your anonymity
       enjoy your privacy
       from probing, prying
       telescopes and space craft
while you can from this preying planet.

For when humans discover more about you
       and they are doing so at a rapid pace,
with the hope
       they can sustain their fragile, fleshy forms
       with air and water
       and recoverable resources,
       after they made a mess on Earth
       or sent sturdy robots to claim your assets
which can further pollute the devastation of Gaia
and her inhabitants and habitat,
       cause Earth's demise
       disturb the galaxy
       perhaps the universe.

So though I am curious about you,
I am content to respect your sovereignty
       whether you have sentient beings or not.

Let Earth's people have the illusion
       they are alone
and unsustainable elsewhere.

Naming Exoplanets

Since 1988 we have discovered
over 2108 planets
in 1350 planetary systems
511 multiple planetary systems
as of April 2016
and more will be discovered
with the launch of James Webb telescope.

Just some of the extra-solar planets
in the Conservative Habitable Zone
with Earth, have garbled name tags,--
words with numbers like
      Gliese 667Cc
      Kepler 446b
      Wolf 1061c
      Kepler 421
      Kepler 186f

Personally, I renamed Kepler 186f
for poet Robert Frost since it is chilly there,
with nicknames for planet and inhabitants:
      Bobby   Bobalongs
      Bobbits   Bobbins
      Frosties,   Frostlings
      Frostbytes,   Frosters
      Bobbines   Bobbles
But I do not think it will catch on
with scientists—and there are
so many exoplanets.   Yet
I am sure we could come up
with enough poets.

We have named billions of people on Earth
and our solar system planets.
But in such a vast multiverse,
naming planets could be a challenge.
We may discover if alien beings
dwell there, they may have
their own names in many languages.

Some uninhabited places will have
to rely on visitors to name them.
What a collision of cosmic languages!
Let's not let galaxies fight wars
over which names should be used.

Someday we might have conferences
on planetary naming, allow many names
or decide on one cosmic name,
agreed on peacefully.

When the time comes, perhaps
we can compile an encyclopedia
of planetary names- all the variations
and nicknames so we can address them
appropriately and set our travel plans
accordingly. Maybe then we can move on
to document:
      comets
      asteroids
      meteors
      space stations
      satellites
with user - friendly names, cosmic correctness.

With our computers advancing so rapidly,
we can put the task to Cosmosnet and robots.
With greater communication with the multiverse,
connecting all matter by naming,
we could become closer to The Great Namer
for those who believe in a Supreme Being
responsible for all of creation.

There are lists of names for God depending
on traditions with 72, 101 or 950 names and more.
Each continent has multiple names for God.
Whatever you call The Source, Prime Creator

Hashem	Adonai	Allah
The Light	Most High	Elohim
YHWH	Yaweh	Yahyah
El-Shaddai	Elah	Ehyeh–I AM
Jehovah	Prabhu	Guru Nanak
Ajok	Imra	Great Gish
Munsin	BaiameImana	
Yala	Mulungu	Bugu

Akai-Purakh–timeless one

Nirankar–formless one....   Or not

I wonder what Unimaginable Sparkling
calls its creations?

Planet X

We may have 9 planets again!
      5,000 times bigger than former planet Pluto
          billions of miles further away.
Scientists think they have found Planet X
      on the fringes of our solar system.

A gas giant almost as big as Neptune
      maybe moons and rings,
          10,000 to 20,000 years to orbit sun.
Scientist predict by mathematical and computer modeling,
      anticipate discovery via telescope within five years.

For the first time in 150 years there is evidence
      the planets in our solar system census is incomplete.
          Pluto is dwarf planet. Planet X will be #9.
Once found there will be no Pluto-style planetary debate.
      Planet X is believed to be ten times more massive than Earth.

Mike Brown, the Pluto Killer is a Planet X advocate,
      says Pluto is a gravitational slave to Neptune
          Planet X dominates its cosmic neighborhood.

But Alan Stern principal scientist for NASA's New Horizon
      spacecraft which flew by Pluto for the first time,
          still sees Pluto as a real–not dwarf planet.
Prediction is not discovery. Planet X or 9 has an egg-shaped orbit.
      Would vary 20-100 billion miles away. Someone might see it.

Predictions are from six objects in the Kuiper Belt
      called the Twilight Zone- far reaches of the solar system.
          They claim orbits are influenced by a big planet.
Pluto is in the Kuiper Belt as well and they found Pluto.
      Sedna, a large minor planet was found there also.

Brown says "We have felt a great disturbance in the force."
      Scientists say they have found the gravitational signature
          of Planet X lurking in the outskirts of our solar system.
If they find Planet X and keep the name beginning with "P" like Pluto,
      all the mnemonics to learning the planets will be the same.

Mythic and Cosmic Pluto

Pluto is kind of a planetary pet
similar to lovable Disney dog.
Demoted to a binary-dwarf planet
with Charon in cosmic catalogue.
> Four moons orbit: bi-lobed Hydra, nebulous Nix.
> blobular Kerboros and mini-satellite Styx.

Similar to lovable Disney dog
not god Pluto's three-headed dog Cerberus,
mysterious mini-planet is getting in dialogue
from data New Horizon spacecraft brought for us.
> 20 atmospheric layers make Pluto hazy.
> Solar winds swarm, flux like crazy.

Demoted to a binary-dwarf planet,
re-defined after larger Eris was found.
People took nine planets for granted.
Then like Pluto Roman god of Underground
> remained mostly unseen. Now viewed,
> this six-body system in Kuiper Belt is previewed.

With Charon in cosmic catalogue,
mythic boatman is paired to god Pluto's world again--
but crater-pitted Pluto where ice clogs.
Pluto has a reddish, gray-white rugged terrain.
> Charon also has complex geology.
> Both more ancient than their mythology.

Four moons orbit: bi-lobed Hydra, nebulous Nix.
The moons suggest water-ice composition.
Perhaps a giant collision was in the mix
to set in place this rotational evolution.
> New Horizon flyby allowed moon-measures,
> high-spatial resolution imaging to treasures.

Blobular Kerboros and mini-satellite Styx
have connections to earthly mythic roots.
River Styx to underworld meant you're in a fix,
found yourself ferried and dead to boot.
> We look at new discoveries, give kudos
> as we gaze and praise again awesome Pluto.

The Dwarf Planets

Pluto is like Snow White
surrounding herself with dwarfs.
Once they called Pluto
a dwarf planet, Pluto's
neighboring planetoids:
trans-Neptunian objects
were designated likewise.

Makemake, Eris, MK2 joined the club
discovered by Hubble Space telescope.
All hang out in the Kuiper Belt.
Many more are bound to follow.
Makemake is the second
brightest icy dwarf planet after Pluto.
Makemake is 100 miles in diameter and black.

Mike Brown the "Pluto Killer"
was not part of this latest
S/2015(136472) or nicknamed
MK2 discovery team. But
he was on Makemake's case.
Each new dwarf planet seems
to keep them in own class of space object.

Lucky we let asteroids and meteorites
be unnamed mostly. Haley had a comet.
All this space debris, stars, planets, moons,
orbiting the cosmos is mind-bursting.
But what about Pluto's moon Charon?
It appears a smaller twin. Charon also gets
an upgrade. How tiny can dwarf planets be?

When Snow White encountered seven dwarfs
with personality descriptive names,
they did her bidding. Does Pluto command
such deference for providing a new category?
Does Pluto communicate with them? If so,
I doubt it would be like Pluto dog to owner.
I'm glad Pluto has company with things in common.

Dwarf Planets Pantoum

While searching the inner Oort Cloud
in the outer edges of the solar system,
dwarf planets reside, hidden in a shroud.
These oddballs have become a hot item.

In the outer edges of the Solar System,
astronomers are excited to find what they seek.
The oddballs have become a hot item.
These objects are numerous, not unique.

Sedna was an early discovery–
small, shiny and red.
Then VP 133, nicknamed Biden from VP
in this wasteland considered dead.

Small, shiny and red
Sedna's flashier than VP's pink.
In a wasteland considered dead,
there are many more dwarfs they think.

These dwarf planets live with comets like ISON,
orbit the inner Oort Cloud with thousands
of similar objects. Much to ponder upon–
part of cosmos' many wonderlands.

Orbit inner Oort Cloud with thousands–
telescopes are finding many more.
Part of cosmos' many wonderlands
almost all Earthlings are eager to explore.

Reviving Bennu

Bennu was a self-created bird being
according to Egyptian myth.
Bennu played role seeing
creation of the world therewith.
       Bennu renewed itself like the sun
       means to shine, rise to brilliance one.

According to Egyptian myth
Bennu is associated with Osiris because
gray heron is symbol of rebirth.
Asteroid Bennu has a new cause.
       NASA's Osiris Rex wants to release
       spacecraft into orbit to snatch Bennu piece.

Bennu played role in seeing
perhaps, early universe. Scientist detected
asteroid Bennu has right composition decreeing
it was close enough to sample, so selected.
       Osiris Rex will launch in September 2016.
       Two years before it reaches Bennu's scene.

Creation of the world therewith
could be revealed when Osiris Rex spacecraft
returns with chunk of Bennu's regolith
providing chemical and organic molecules to draft.
       Does Bennu carry elements, precursors for life?
       Was Earth seeded by asteroids, Earth's midwife?

Bennu renewed itself like the sun
once worshipped, now heron species extinct.
With asteroid Bennu, a new rebirth has begun.
Return of discovery of creational instinct?
       Bennu was chosen for possible life-giving resources,
       so scientists can learn more about cosmic forces.

Means to shine, rise to brilliance one,
Bennu-bird called "Lord of Jubilees"
Bennu-asteroid part of early creation?
Bringer of Earth's birds and bees?
       Asteroid Bennu could collide with Earth.
       Take bite of us. We seek another berth?

Catching a Dragon

Orbiting 250 miles above Earth,
a robotic arm from the International Space Station
grabbed a SpaceX Dragon cargo ship
carrying 7,000 pounds of freight
to supply the spacecraft.

BEAM- Bigelow Expandable Activity Module
will remain attached until the hatch
opens for the six member crew
to do their tests and sensor swaps.
Dreamers have big plans for BEAM.

NASA envisions inflatable habitats on Mars.
SpaceX chief Elon Musk wants to establish
a city on Mars. They recycle boosters
landing on a solid platform at sea to save money
for more access for more people to more places.

Bigelow Aerospace hopes to launch
a pair of inflatable space stations
in four years for commercial lease.
Earthlings are moving skyward- bubbling
the cosmos with tourists and residents.

Space is a vast and turbulent place.
We must find a way to nourish our DNA.
Hybrids and robots are sturdier star stuff.
Scientists hope to implant memories
and consciousness into robots, save us a trip.

If we are immortal souls leaving bodies behind,
change host-vehicles for different dimensions–
why not let a robot explore and report
where it is difficult for flesh to go without terraforming
outside our transplanted habitats.

Maybe our next life gig will be as a conscious robot,
maybe one implanted with our earthly memories.
Whether formless or in form, dreamers
will chase dragons, reach for stars
long after humanity's bubbles burst.

Another Dawning of the Age of Aquarius

When the moon is in the seventh house
And Jupiter aligns with Mars
And peace will guide the planets
And love will steer the stars
This is the dawning of the Age of Aquarius...
From song lyrics of "Aquarius"

An ultracool dwarf star named Trappist -1
for the Belgian TRAPPIST telescope in Chile
is unusually small, reddish, one-eighth of our sun,
40 light years away and cooler with three planets.
The size of Jupiter, it is located
in the constellation Aquarius.

Three un-named, exoplanets
appear to be temperate. We hope to hunt
for signs of life with NASA's Spitzer Telescope.
The Hubble Telescope will join in search soon.
These planets might be habitable to us.
Maybe some other life forms as well.

From planets, Trappist-1 looks like a stationary red ball.
Closest planet orbits in about one and a half days.
All three planets have one side facing the star.
One side is frigid and one side torrid.
In between regions might be comfortable–for us.
They appear to be Earth-sized.

These planets remind scientists of GJ 1214b
which has an exotic cloud cover with unknown elements.
Twice the size of Earth, like the dynamic trio
GJ has the scientists' attention and warrants more study.
Soon James Webb Space Telescope can spy water, ozone
and carbon dioxide–ingredients for life–for us.

Scientists did not think ultracool dwarf stars
had planets. Now a new area of investigation
for the search for extraterrestrial life.
If we did discover life forms there, how
would we interact? Would we have learned
from the devastation we caused Earth?

Two Sides of the Moon

The moon is a two-faced Janus,
　　　light and dark, yin and yang.

Human touchdowns on the light-side
　　　leave footprints, find dust toxic.

There is controversy if we ever landed.
　　　More controversy about the dark side.

Speculation of alien compounds on the surface
and within the moon which some say rings like a bell.

If it is a hollow spaceship with magnetic qualities,
to tug tides, we hope the moon stays in orbit.

But if the moon leaves Earth, a magic spell,
fantasies will spin into the cosmos.

When I see the pocked light-side,
I wonder about the dark-side.

What do the space telescopes see
and what are they willing to tell us?

If we plan to exploit the moon, perhaps we better
know if other beings got there first.

Moon's mysteries unsolved.
Some facts. Many theories.

How attached are we to the moon
and how attached is the moon to us?

Interplanetary Immigration

Mars Interplanetary Immigration Director:
Speaks to Members of the Martian Assembly

I would like to propose we review
our Interplanetary Immigration Policy and Protocols.
Earth is planning to send an expedition
to establish a colony on our planet.
They have selected 22 volunteers to come
and have advanced their technology
and inflatable habitats to do so.
They want to terraform and create cities.

Already they have aerial surveillance
and have placed vehicles on our surface
to test the viability of their exodus.
They litter with the dysfunctional discards.
Their lack of stewardship of Earth
necessitates the need for other places
to host life: exoplanets, solar system planets
and they want to send nanocrafts
to Alpha Centauri to seek escape routes
when they destroy their planet.
They discovered moon dust is toxic
to people and their machines- so we
are the closest hope for survival and exploitation.

What can we do to protect our indigenous population
as well as our environment
from this invasive species?
They plan to exploit the planet's resources
for commercial purposes and as a tourist attraction.
They will bring disease, destructive beliefs,
violent tendencies, usurp resources,
having not evolved to where
our underground residents have achieved.

What are our cosmic obligations?
How are we to deal with this onslaught?
Are we to remain passive?
Use peaceful protocols as we suffer
the consequences of their breach of our boundaries?
How have aliens been treated elsewhere in the galaxy?
Earth's UN protocols to deal with aliens
might not work here. Must we accept this delivery?

Breakthrough Starshot

We commit to the next great leap into the cosmos, because we are human and our nature is to fly. Stephen Hawking

Breakthrough Starshot brings scientists and visionaries
together to launch light beams, light sails, lightest spacecraft
on a mission to Alpha Centauri within a generation.

The project was announced on the 55th anniversary
of Russian Yuri Gagarin's first human in space flight.
Russian Internet investor Yuri Milner is named for him.

Milner wants to send hundreds or thousands
of tiny spacecraft weighing less than an ounce
to explore the Alpha Centauri Star system.

Breakthrough Starshot focuses on detection
of Earth-like planets and alien signals. They will fund
the development of light-propelled, nanocraft-spaceships.

Pushed by force of light-particles, shoved by laser arrays
maybe these nanocraft can sense habitable conditions
for life in our closest neighboring star system.

The search for extra-terrestrial intelligence
by terrestrial intelligence will take our best minds
and millions in investments focused outward not here.

These tiny, light-powered satellites called Light Sail
envisioned by Carl Sagan, Bill Nye, the Planetary Society
are under-development and might take flight in a few years.

But to get to Alpha Centauri they need advancements in speed,
nanotechnology to create incredibly light solar sails to carry craft.
We need very light sails and very big lasers for it to be a go.

Advances in electronic miniaturization, laser technology
and fabrication of thin and light materials make this mission
a possibility. Tiny spacecraft would be boosted by rocket and freed.

Meanwhile back on Earth, we face climate change, upheavals--
natural and caused by people and their technologies.
We already have space junk to contend with in near-Earth orbit.

Still, I am starry-eyed, cosmically-curious. Let's take a starshot.
It might provide an exit route from a polluted, plundered planet
when we have nowhere else to go but up.

Milkandromeda

In five billion years Andromeda and Milky Way
are expected to merge. Theories say
they could just pass through or they may

form one Milkandromeda galaxy, but
(the probability is not the scuttlebutt)
we have not cracked this cosmic nut.

In the center could be SuperMassive Black Hole
with capacity to swallow both galaxies whole?
That is more than most sentient beings can thole.

Current ideas might need some revision
after colossal four-galaxy collision.
We're considering two. Have no decision.

Stars rarely do collide.
The distances between are wide,
yet our doubts don't subside.

All the universe has vibrations?
Any help in these situations?
Have we made calibrations?

Vibrations can be considered pitch?
Brain turns vibes to music which
to me sounds very eldritch.

To some this appears
to be music of the spheres
translated in our brain and ears.

Milkandromeda is in no hurry.
I will not waste time with worry.
There are other ways for Earth to bury.

Some theories remain a mystery.
Totally bewildering to me.
But I'm fascinated stellarly.

In A Galaxy Far, Far Away

Near Ursa Major astronomers found
        GN-211 beyond Hubble Space Telescope's
                limits to observe this most distant galaxy.

GN-211 seems small, reddish
        and unexpectedly bright with light
                leaving the galaxy 13.4 billion years ago.

Scientists think the universe is 13.8 billion years old.
        This galaxy is from when the universe
                was about 3 percent of what is now.

EGSY8p7 was the previous
        distant record holder, but light from GN-211
                is 200 million years closer to Big Bang.

Scientists proclaim this is the best view
        of conditions of the Dark Ages of Universe
                when cosmos was opaque, no stars or quasars.

Hubble allows peeks at cosmic past
        beyond what they expected to see. Some day
                somewhere a galaxy even further away?

An International team found GN-211
        combining talents and equipment globally.
                We could discover more galaxies and multiverses

lurking in dark universal vastness
        beckoning our multiversal understanding
                of sacred geometry, curiosity and imagination.

Super Massive Black Holes

Super massive black holes remain hidden,
some by quasars at galactic centers. When bidden

they nibble stars, gas and clouds.
Big gulps of whole galaxies allowed
when in feeding stage to suck in whole crowd.

Scientists say they have solved their theories,
have math to prove their quasi-queries.

Now our Milky Way's center isn't aggressively feeding.
Becoming its diet is not what we're needing.

Early experiments were tech-flaw ridden.
Super massive black holes remain hidden.

Scientist feel they have solved their theories
after years at their telescopes for series
of observations. Beyond event horizon–still eerie.

What's on the other end could be worse
or maybe lead to another universe?

Stelliferous

And through the uncurtained window
Falls the waste light of stars.   Lola Ridge

We live in the Stelliferous Era
the Age of the Anthropocene.
People can still stare at stars.
Despite polluted skies, stars are seen.

Pundits predict eons to come
the stars will eventually snuff out.
People will have pulled last curtains.
Darkness will prevail....no doubt.

Even if we survive to be interstellar
and enjoy starlit beacons in our flight,
at some point it will be curtains
for our universal starry plight.

There is no waste of starlight
with windows open, eye on sky.
For this part of the universe...
stars are in frabjous supply.

I peer out my window
at shimmering lights, behold
star stuff's mystery...
uncurtained from the cold.

Outerknown

Outerknown: destination haven't dreamed of yet and maybe doesn't exist.
Pushing known limits.

The outerknown sparks my imagination
lures my curiosity to fascinating paths.
I may not know my next destination,
contemplate the aftermaths.
      I want to explore unafraid
      what the cosmos played.

Lures my curiosity to fascinating paths
to push boundaries, peek outside the box.
With limited equipment, lack of higher maths
I still pursue the unorthodox.
      Guess I am a day and night dreamer,
      trying to be a manifesting schemer.

I may not know my next destination
in what dimension or universe,
but in times of earthly frustration
I figure I might not be worse.
      The possibilities of the outerknown,
      I want to find out on my own.

Contemplate the aftermaths
of any explorations,
could nail me to rigid laths,
create fearful intimidations.
      Not knowing, living in ambiguity
      means being devoid of certainty.

I want to explore unafraid
but conditions make me fearful.
All the violence, distance displayed,
presents quite an earful.
      My senses tend to overwhelm.
      when I imagine another realm.

What the cosmos played
from the dance of creation
leaves me quite dismayed
when I attempt speculation.
      But I remain resolute, undeterred,
      seek any outerknown clues offered.

Acknowledgments

To learn to read is to light a fire; every syllable
that is spelled out is a spark. Victor Hugo

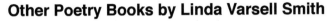

Other Poetry Books by Linda Varsell Smith

Cinqueries: A Cluster of Cinquos and Lanterns
Fibs and Other Truths
Black Stars on a White Sky
Poems That Count
Poems That Count Too
Winging It: New and Selected Poems
Red Cape Capers: Playful Backyard Meditations
Star Stuff: A Soul- Splinter Experiences the Cosmos
Light-Headed: A Soul-Splinter Experiences Light

Chapbooks

Being Cosmic
Intra-Space Chronicles
Light-Headed

On-Line Web-Site Books
Free Access @ www.rainbowcommunications.org

Syllable of Velvet
Word-Playful
Poetluck

Anthologies

The Second Genesis
Branches
Poetic License
Poetic License 2015
Jubilee

Gillian Wigmore is the author of two other books of poems: *soft geography* (Caitlin Press, 2007), winner of the 2008 ReLit Award, and *Dirt of Ages* (Nightwood Editions, 2012). She is also the author of a novella, *Grayling* (Mother Tongue Publishing, 2014). Her work has been published in magazines, shortlisted for prizes and anthologized. She lives in Prince George, BC.